THE ROMANTIC BODY
Love and Sexuality in Keats, Wordsworth, and Blake

The Romantic Body

*Love and Sexuality
in Keats, Wordsworth,
and Blake*

BY JEAN H. HAGSTRUM

THE UNIVERSITY OF TENNESSEE PRESS
KNOXVILLE

The paper in this book meets the guidelines for permanence
and durability of the Committee on Production Guidelines
for Book Longevity of the Council on Library Resources.
Binding materials have been chosen for durability.

Library of Congress Cataloging in Publication Data

Hagstrum, Jean H.
    The Romantic Body: Love and sexuality in Keats,
Wordsworth, and Blake
    Bibliography: p.
    Includes index.
    1. English poetry—19th century—History and
criticism.   2. Romanticism—England.   3. Love in
literature.   4. Sex in literature.   5. Keats, John,
1795–1821—Criticism and interpretation.   6. Wordsworth,
William, 1770–1850—Criticism and interpretation.
7. Blake, William, 1757–1827—Criticism and interpretation.   I. Title.
PR590.H28   1985   821'.7'09354   85-7485
ISBN 0-87049-482-1

For

Elaine Kauvar   Jeffry Spencer

PREFACE AND ACKNOWLEDGMENTS

This is a small book on a large subject. The subject is large because it is central to Romantic thought and expression and also because so far relatively little has been done on its purely human aspects. The book is small because the John C. Hodges Lectures at the University of Tennessee are confined to three only (I have added in publication an additional chapter and an Epilogue) and because, for major Romantic authors I have not chosen to write about at length, my subject has been treated authoritatively. I refer to Anthony John Harding's book on Coleridge and to Nathaniel Brown's on Shelley; reference will be made later to both books. More consideration needs to be given to love and sexuality in Byron. I have myself made a beginning in a piece on Byron and Edleston in the *Festschrift* for James Osborn (see my Bibliographical Essay), and I intend to say something in the future about the love of Haidée and Juan in *Don Juan*.

Because of such work, I do not by any means feel that I am on a desert island when writing about Romantic love and sexuality; but I can understand something of Schopenhauer's sense of loneliness when he said in "The Metaphysics of the Love of the Sexes," a chapter in *The World as Will and Idea*: "I have no predecessors"; the subject has "practically been disregarded by the philosophers altogether." And this subject, Schopenhauer thought and I too think, has been the chief theme of dramatic, narrative, and lyrical literature, classical and romantic, Western and Eastern, and may, in its very nature, be unequalled by any other in interest and importance. Even though I disagree profoundly with this philosopher's narrowness of approach and with the severe etiological restrictions he lays upon his subject, I must say at the outset that he has provided the basic orientation and emphasis of my treatment. He believed that love, however ethereal its aspiration and reach, is "rooted in the sexual impulse alone," love being only a "more definitely determined, specialized, and . . . individualized sexual impulse."

One can sympathize with Byron's desire regarding the hero of the work that made him famous: "I much wish to avoid identifying Childe Harold's character with mine" (*Byron LJ.*, II, 75–76). I trust that I am sufficiently aware that pressures from the author's psyche on his art come in subtle and diverse ways and, though they leave deep marks, that these

vii

are also elusive and strange. And when they are mixed with pressures from contemporary culture and from artistic traditions, they become nuanced and complex indeed. Consider how much would have to go into a proper evaluation of Byron on marriage, for example, or how much lies behind Gibbon's famous remark, "I sighed as a lover; I obeyed as a son." The historian Lawrence Stone, to whom we all owe so much on the subject of love, marriage, sexuality, and the family, has been rightly seen as being here somewhat one-dimensional in viewing this exclamation of Gibbon as an illustration of generational conflict, in which new forms of mating arrangements clash with the old. Harry C. Payne isolates some of the complications: Gibbon was less than eager to marry, he welcomed familial disapproval, and he was here doing "an artful psychological dance among critical norms"—norms, one must add, that are purely literary and even Petrarchan as well as cultural in the broader sense. A clever and cultivated bachelor will know how to cover shyness or abnormality with the stereotypes of civilization.

Amid such complexities we must make choices of course, and I do not want to obscure the direction in which I face. It remains the same in this book as in my recent study of seventeenth- and eighteenth-century love, *Sex and Sensibility*, which Patricia Meyer Spacks has said, accurately, "rests on the assumption that we can learn something important about literature (and painting and music) by investigating rather than deploring its subject matter." Professor Spacks goes on to make a distinction, also accurate, between my work and that of the late Paul de Man, whom I admired greatly as a subtle student of language, rhetoric, and literary form and also as a quite marvelous unraveller of poetic skeins, especially Romantic ones: "'If you want to talk about men,' Paul de Man remarked at the English Institute, 'you're in the wrong field. We talk about letters.' Hagstrum talks about men and women and their representations. He thus claims his field as a domain of the human, subordinating interest in language to concentration on language's referents."

Separated from so distinguished a thinker as de Man, I fancy I see an emphasis sympathetic or at least similar to mine in a passage of the *Prelude* (1805: VI, 117–34, *Prel.*, 192), where Wordsworth asserts that the books he had loved the most at Cambridge were still "dearest" to him:

> for, being versed
> In living Nature, I had there a guide
> Which opened frequently my eyes, else shut.

He then confesses he was at that time verbally ruled "by the trade in classic niceties"—

> by that overprized
> And dangerous craft of picking phrases out
> From languages that want the living voice.

I do not wish to accuse any scholar or critic now writing of commerce in a jejune linguistic classicism unnourished by life and experience, but I do take to heart Wordsworth's warning that language alone (and it does not have to be a "dead" one) should not be transformed to nature,

> To tell us what is passion, what is truth,
> What reason, what simplicity and sense.

I of course try to avoid making an equivalence of nature and art; but, like Wordsworth or, for that matter, Samuel Johnson, I feel the constant need for the mind of the critic to move back and forth between reality and imaginative structures—"From earth to man, from man to earth," as it were.

That "earth" or reality, as the pages that follow will try to show, often includes the poet's psyche and his vital situation and also the artistic tradition, as well as the cultural milieu, that influenced him. I do not pretend to have solved the age-old dilemma of where to place imaginative structures on the life-art axis, nor do I wish even to raise the question of whether art is, finally, greater or less than life. If at times I seem to reach out for actual experience behind the veil of literary imaginings, I suppose this is the result of the orientation which I am here disclosing. I recall a conversation many years ago between two scholarly friends of mine, one a lover of documentation and biography, the other a commentator who kept his Chicago eye fixed firmly on the text. The latter said it was good that we know as little as we do about Shakespeare because we can concentrate more easily on the plays themselves. Whereupon the former expressed the fervent hope that if our friend should discover a personal diary of Shakespeare's thoughts and activities kept shortly before the production of the great tragedies, he would not destroy it. I have found myself through the years longing for as much information about poets' minds and experiences as one can possibly get. Recent critical thought about Richardson's great novel, *Clarissa,* has suggested that the literary artifact to be confronted is not always or simply the first or final edition but, as in this case, *all* the editions and revisions as well as letters to and from the author about the making of the work. Such a view of a literary event enriches criticism by enlarging vision as surely as it creates messy complexities.

In other words, I am confident that the frequent glances I make in the ensuing pages to authors' lives predispose us to respond to zones of verbal energy and do not finally divert attention from the proper locus of critical attention, the work itself. That work I find to be best when its mythic beings and events convey real experience within fictional, rhetorical, and verbal structures. Its worth is finally ratified when it too becomes a part of experience and so presses upon the psyches of later readers and creators.

I thank Theresa Kelley for having read the entire manuscript. I hope it was not a "trial" for her to apply her learning, judgment, and taste to a draft of this work and to contribute insights and even verbal constructions to the final version; but in any case I "acquit" her of responsibility for the errors and failures that remain. I am also grateful to Professor Nancy M. Goslee, who was a lively member of my audience at the University of Tennessee and who has read the entire manuscript — much to its improvement, without incurring any guilt for its continuing deficiencies. My colleagues in the English Department and the Library of Northwestern University, particularly Lawrence Lipking, David Simpson, and Richard Wendorf, have provided stimulation and information during the years, and colleagues and audiences at the University of Tennessee, where many of these pages were delivered in lectures, were courteous, friendly, and intellectually provocative. Beth Darlington has been helpful and encouraging in correspondence about Wordsworth.

I also wish to thank James Thorpe, former director of the Huntington Library and Art Gallery, and its fellows and readers for providing mental stimulation during the tenure of a recent fellowship in San Marino. Once again I acknowledge a debt to the group of professors from all over the country who studied with me for an academic year at Northwestern University under Fellowships in Residence for College Teachers, awarded by the National Endowment for the Humanities. Kathleen Beckerman has done her typically skillful work in "word-processing" my difficult typescript and making corrections. I am grateful to her and to the staff of the University of Tennessee Press for cooperation and assistance.

The two scholars to whom this book is dedicated, quondam collaborators in Blakean and Romantic research of which the ensuing pages constituted a projected part, will individually and together know how deeply I am indebted to them.

CONTENTS

ILLUSTRATIONS

Plate

ABBREVIATIONS

(Full listings appear in the Bibliographical Essay)

Amer.	William Blake, *America*
BCPW.	*Lord Byron: The Complete Poetical Works,* ed. Jerome J. McGann
Byron LJ.	*Byron's Letters and Journals,* ed. Leslie A. Marchand
Coll. Letters	*Collected Letters of Samuel Taylor Coleridge,* ed. Earl Leslie Griggs
Coll. Works	*The Collected Works of Samuel Taylor Coleridge,* general ed., Kathleen Coburn
CP.	*John Keats: Complete Poetry,* ed. Jack Stillinger
CPWC.	*The Complete Poetical Works of Coleridge,* ed. Ernest Hartley Coleridge
E.	*The Complete Poetry and Prose of William Blake,* ed. David V. Erdman
FZ.	William Blake, *The Four Zoas*
Home at Grasmere	William Wordsworth, *Home at Grasmere,* ed. Beth Darlington
Jer.	William Blake, *Jerusalem*
Letters Early	*The Letters of William and Dorothy Wordsworth: The Early Years,* ed. Ernest de Selincourt
LK.	*The Letters of Keats,* ed. Hyder Edward Rollins
Letters Middle	*The Letters of William and Dorothy Wordsworth: The Middle Years,* Part II, ed. Ernest de Selincourt
Love Letters	*The Love Letters of William and Dorothy Wordsworth,* ed. Beth Darlington
MHH.	William Blake, *The Marriage of Heaven and Hell*
Notebooks	*The Notebooks of Samuel Taylor Coleridge,* ed. Kathleen Coburn
Prel.	William Wordsworth, *The Prelude 1799, 1805, 1850,* ed. Jonathan Wordsworth *et al.*
Prose	*The Prose Works of William Wordsworth,* ed. W.J.B. Owen and Jane Worthington Smyser
PW.	*The Poetical Works of William Wordsworth,* ed. Ernest de Selincourt and Helen Darbishire

Salisbury Plain	*The Salisbury Plain Poems of William Wordsworth,* ed. Stephen Gill
SPW.	*Shelley: Poetical Works,* ed. Thomas Hutchinson
Symbol	Leopold Damrosch, Jr., *Symbol and Tradition in Blake's Myth*
VDA.	William Blake, *The Visions of the Daughters of Albion*

THE ROMANTIC BODY
Love and Sexuality in Keats, Wordsworth, and Blake

'And vital feelings of delight
Shall rear her form to stately height,
Her virgin bosom swell.'
Wordsworth, "Three years she grew," *PW.*, II, 215

*. . . Vice . . . is a Negative — . . . we who are philosophers ought
not to call the Staminal Virtues of Humanity by the same name that
we call the omissions of intellect springing from poverty.*
Blake, Annotations to Lavater, *E.*, 601

*. . . there are
Richer entanglements, enthralments far
More self-destroying, leading, by degrees,
To the chief intensity: the crown of these
Is made of love and friendship, and sits high
Upon the forehead of humanity.
All its more ponderous and bulky worth
Is friendship, whence there ever issues forth
A steady splendour; but at the tip-top,
There hangs by unseen film, an orbed drop
Of light, and that is love.*
Keats, *Endymion*, I, 797–807, CP., 83–84

1. INTRODUCTION
Love's Body and Soul

Love, now a universal birth,
From heart to heart is stealing,
From earth to man, from man to earth:
—It is the hour of feeling . . .

And from the blessed power that rolls
About, below, above,
We'll frame the measure of our souls:
They shall be tuned to love.
Wordsworth, "To My Sister," PW., IV, 60

Love rules the court, the camp, the grove,
And man below and saints above,
For love is heaven, and heaven is love.
Walter Scott, The Lay of the Last Minstrel, III.ii

M. H. Abrams has found the chief Romantic values to be "life, love, liberty, hope, and joy." The greatest of these, he believes, is life, "the ground-concept," "itself the highest good, the residence and measure of other goods." The selection of *life* as the Romantic *summum bonum* is understandable, one I find especially congenial because it relates art to nature and to the empirical eighteenth century, from which too often it has been divorced. But my own choice for the quintessential Romantic noun would have been *love,* and the close analyses of poetic passages in the pages that follow are intended to support that choice. The exalted place I give to love is not based primarily on a straightforward, uncomplicated acceptance of the Romantic belief that love is a "light from heaven" or on Frederick L. Beaty's view that in the early nineteenth century love, along with the imagination, was conceived as coming down from on high. Love's priority arose precisely from its forceful presence in nature and man, a fact that should always be borne in mind when encountering the Romantic poets at their most transcendent. No one made more exalted claims for love than Shelley in *Prometheus Unbound*:

> Fate, Time, Occasion, Chance and Change? to these,
> All things are subject but eternal Love.
[II.iv. 119–20, SPW., 238]

But no one was clearer than Shelley about the persistence of human passion—even when man is conceived of as totally free from national, social, or religious constraint:

> the king
> Over himself; just, gentle, wise: but man
> Passionless?—no, yet free from guilt or pain.
>
> [III.iv. 196–98, *SPW.*, 253]

The Body in Romantic Poetry and Art

> *Sexual intercourse began*
> *In nineteen sixty-three*
> *(Which was rather late for me)*—
> *Between the end of the* Chatterly *ban*
> *And the Beatles' first LP.*
>
> Philip Larkin, "Annus Mirabilis"

The celebration of sexual pleasure and the sense of having discovered it belong to many periods; yet more widespread approval of feelings of physical delight seems to me to have existed during the late eighteenth and early nineteenth centuries than at any other time. We should consider how basic and primal in literary criticism are the concepts of pleasure and passion and how great a revision this centrality was of the traditional primacy given to instruction. And we must consider also that *pleasure* almost inevitably carried connotations of physical love. Samuel Johnson said, "When we talk of pleasure, we mean sensual pleasure. When a man says, he had pleasure with a woman, he does not mean conversation, but something of a very different nature." And James Boswell said that "the word *Pleasure* . . . commonly suggests at first the idea of sensual gratification, . . . We all know what is meant by a Man of Pleasure, or a Woman of Pleasure." It is one of the purposes of this book to keep alive these fundamental meanings without, however, confining them to heterosexual congress. Erasmus Darwin, whose biological, botanical, and generally scientific poetry influenced much Romantic language, continually assigns an extended physical meaning to *pleasure* and related words like *sensibility* and *delight.* For example, in *Zoonomia* (1796) he says that "the first most lively impression of pleasure that the infant enjoys after its nativity, is excited by the odours of its mother's milk" (xvi.8.3), and he finds serenity in the smile that relaxes the mouth after the fatigues of sucking (xvi.8.4). It is remarkable how many of the dreams and fantasies recorded in Coleridge's *Notebooks* seem to be recollections of just such pleasures as these.

4

A culture in which the sensual and the sensuous are deeply rooted will inevitably and appropriately find visual expression, and it is therefore not amiss to provide a brief *tour d'horizon* with respect to the sister art of painting in England. If one surveys the whole field of Romantic painting, one is not overwhelmed with the frequency of erotic subjects. But frequency should not be confused with intensity, and three English painters, two of them not very well known, are often intensely physical. Henry Fuseli (1741–1825), an immigrant to England, brought with him Continental storm, stress, and sensuality. Blake was pleased and highly receptive, but Coleridge dubbed him "Fuzzle" or "Fuzzly" and called him "a Brusher up of Convulsia & Tetanus* upon innocent Canvas" (*Notebooks,* no. 954 and note). There is no need here to discuss his sensual Dido or his several *Nightmares,* but we must note that Fuseli ranged from a delight in normal healthy love to perverse and tortured love — a range in love resembling what Coleridge confided to his *Notebooks.* Fuseli eroticizes typically English themes and traditions and thereby becomes an important analogue to native English poets, whose hidden erotic strains he thus helps to bring out. He makes the haughty modish woman of so much English portrait art strangely and perversely sensual, and in eerie and suggestive ways feminizes social scenes, combining realism and irrationality, the proud ego with the carnal id. (See Plate I.) It is not only that the clothes cover obviously lascivious bodies but that the clothes themselves are charged with sexual, often perversely sexual, electricity.

Rakishness at least carries over into his illustrations of *The Merry Wives of Windsor,* and the painter again and again gives us an erotic Shakespeare — for example, when Titania kisses Bottom — though he often toned down the physicality when he came to illustrate the large Shakespeare editions, where it became rather delicate and coquettish than brutally direct or overt. Even the chaste Spenser is not spared erotic titillations in the illustrations; and, as Frederick Antal points out, in the 1790s, precisely when Fuseli was under the influence of Milton's sublimity, the erotic becomes more prominent than ever. He should not be seen as only approximating the remote but also, and perhaps more importantly, as freshening the familiar and somewhat dry English soil with erotic dew.

James Barry (1741–1806) — like Fuseli an influence on Blake, who angrily and eloquently defended this much misunderstood and maligned painter whose "grasp of mind" Samuel Johnson had praised — also eroti-

---

*The word comes from the Greek for spasm. OED gives an eighteenth-century citation that associates it with swooning fits and distractions.

5

PLATE I. Henry Fuseli, Illustration of Cowper, engraved by Rhodes.

cized Milton and Shakespeare. He eroticized Milton by making Sin a highly sexual but, with her monstrous breasts, also an unpersuasive creature, and he eroticized Shakespeare by giving to the dead Cordelia's body in two fine paintings (without sacrificing her modesty) a touch of the erotic in her pliant limbs and even a hint of the post-coital in the undulations of hair and drapery. Since sexualized mythology is so prominent in the early Keats, we should notice the same phenomenon in Barry. His *Venus Rising from the Sea,* exhibited 1772 (Plate II), portrays a girl who is fresh, young, virginal and alluring, even though the face is in profile and "steam" or spray covers the pudenda like a gauze. She is Venus, of course, of the Andyomene type, but she can be said to represent the love emanating from young innocence that we shall see moved most Romantic poets. Barry himself must have felt her appeal, which he apparently desired to emphasize: Cupid, having shot an arrow, looks at you, dear spectator, as though you are indeed his intended victim.

How different is the much later (1804) oil on canvas entitled *Jupiter and Juno on Mount Ida* (Plate III), a ponderous but exciting rendition, far above the titillating eroticism of some of the painter's contemporaries. Juno, with a dignified Roman nose, nevertheless has an erotic eye, large breasts, and bodily rhythms that only the fleshly undulations of the father of the gods can match. The two large bodies, marvellously rounded, roll in waves of powerful desire while both his and her hands remain delicate. It is not inappropriate to notice that here we have a married pair, reminding us, despite the usual reputation of the Olympian pantheon for hanky-panky, of the insistent union in eighteenth-century sensibility of *wedded* love and the erotic. It is significant that so powerfully a sexual painting as this does, like so much in Romantic poetry, invoke conjugal love. If we consider Barry's *Venus* and his *Jupiter-Juno* together—the one virginal, the other heartily but legally amorous—we can discern a stunning reversal of Swift's famous disjunction of the attractive but poisonously disruptive Venus from the shrewish and ungracious Juno.*

William Etty (1787–1849) is at least a generation younger than Fuseli and Barry and can be said to extend the erotic into the Victorian period. It is precisely because of his obsession with the female nude body that he has been thought to have "no parallel in English painting"; and it has also been said that "no other British artist . . . has painted the nude

---

*"VENUS, a beautiful good-natured Lady, was the Goddess of Love; *Juno,* a terrible Shrew, the Goddess of Marriage; and they were always mortal Enemies" ("Thoughts on Various Subjects" in *Prose Works,* ed. Herbert Davis [Oxford: Basil Blackwell, 1962], IV, 247).

PLATE II. James Barry, *Venus Rising from the Sea.*

PLATE III. James Barry, *Jupiter and Juno on Mount Ida.*

with such devotion and mastery, and invested her with such voluptuous vitality." There can of course be no doubt of the delicately sensual appeal created in nude after nude by this painter, a formally uneducated product of a strict and impecunious Wesleyan upbringing. Alexander Gilchrist, biographer of Etty as well as Blake, stated in 1855 what would have been the Romantic defense of Etty's libidinous power had it been made a half century earlier: "It is glowing Nature he gives us . . . sympathizingly and faithfully interpreted by a mind itself vivid and glowing. And Nature is itself no ascetic." Gilchrist discloses the source of Etty's power: it lies in his reality, the uncompromising sexual reality of the women he portrays even when they appear in mythologies. His *Reclining Female Nude* breaks with the convention of concealing the pudenda, by raising a leg to expose rather than cover her pubic hair, and that action supports the realism that the large, naturalistically painted breasts also enforce. *Mars, Venus and Attendant* (a late painting, 1840) touches on one of Etty's favorite mythic subjects, but it is far from formulaic. Partly an outdoor scene—the bed is under a Roman arch—it is one of the most sensual "actions" ever portrayed in English art: Venus, attended by a black girl, has only partly put on a shift that covers about half of her genitalia, as she looks down on the sleeping Mars in a mood of post-coital melancholy. Another Venus (Plate IV; for it the painter used the conventional title, *Toilet of Venus*) is, however, far from conventional in the representation: there is no looking-glass, there is neither Cupid nor an attendant, and there is very little idealization. Looking to one side, Venus strains her neck-muscles realistically, not beautifully, and the humble face—perhaps that of a working-girl model—has a look of human mystery about it. The *Standing Female Nude* at the Sheffield City Art Gallery is also realistic but in a different way. Not totally successful or fully compelling, the frontal, full-breasted, large-limbed portrayal, with the girl's eyes lowered suggestively, is nevertheless another example of Etty's honest realism. That realism can also encompass delicacy and virginal timidity: *The Bather* (Plate V)—a version of Susannah and the Elders, even though more immediately it may represent James Thomson's Musidora—presents a nude standing in water, unregarded as she peers intently at the bank, as shy as she is lovely, her body curved like that of the Venus Pudica. And so we come back, despite the Venereal allusion, to the essentially nubile woman, that exciting combination of beauty and modesty. The insistent suggestion of the nudes of Etty, as of so much contemporary expression in all media, is that eroticism is most alluring when it is redolent of the domestic nest.

Fuseli grew out of German *Sturm und Drang* and brought with him to England some of its disrupting tensions; but none of the painters

PLATE IV. William Etty, *The Toilet of Venus.*

PLATE V. William Etty, *Musidora: the Bather "at the Doubtful Breeze Alarmed."*

we have so far discussed presents sexuality in a really revolutionary context, though such art can be thought of as softening and so preparing sensibility to accept change. The body, however, often served directly as the symbol of and the force for social and political revision, some of it even violent. H.L. Mencken called revolution "the sex of politics," and many contemporary writers saw the great upheavals in France and the Romantic reactions to them as being examples of sexual excess. One reason for not including Thomas Rowlandson in our discussion of painting is that his art at its most erotically suggestive was largely produced when he was old and cold, when he found that safety came only "from the king, from God, from a father, from a muse, from a statue of Venus, and from Sir Joshua." Even Edmund Burke, the hostile commentator on matters French, saw that energetic youthfulness was a prime characteristic of revolution. Ronald Paulson has called "the act of love" the "quintessential act of rebellion in patriarchal society." It was surely not merely coincidental that in England, as the revolutionary 1780s moved into the 1790s, it became commercially profitable for even the vendors of small literary wares "to expose certain pamphlets in shop windows and upon stalls in alleys and thorough-fares, which, if any police was kept up in this great capital, would be put down by the civil magistrate as a public nuisance." The author of these words, Richard Cumberland, was referring among other things to the indecently illustrated and highly detailed accounts, verbatim, of adultery trials.

Neither art nor lurid documentary writing bore the powerfully disruptive force of some Gothic fiction. The Marquis de Sade, who, if any one did, surely knew what he was talking about in this area, praised Matthew G. Lewis's *The Monk* and called its appearance "truly a literary event." He even found that this genre of writing "was the inevitable outcome of the revolutionary upheavals experienced throughout the whole of Europe." *The Monk* (1796) and the earlier *Vathek* (1786) of William Beckford both need to be examined as examples of revolutionary sexuality. Precisely because *Vathek* is the extravagant and lurid fiction that it is, it can be regarded as a symptom of a revolutionary change in sexual mores. That change both sprang from and itself caused psychic disturbance within, its very breaches of decorum in taste and literary structure permitting glimpses into subjective depths individual and collective. Its basic theme, forbidden knowledge, includes the sexual. And what a procession of perversions we encounter: the vampire mother, surrounded with her black maids of honor, who loves dead bodies and strange odors; the delicately similar cousins, so like figures from a Canova sculpture, who embrace and kiss in a dalliance that suggests brother-sister incest; the royal son who builds a palace to each of the five senses;

13

the baleful halls of the Eblis with their mummies and bones and with their horrible convulsions and screams, which yet make gorgeously rich appeals to appetite and sense. It helps us identify the limits of Romantic sensibility if we observe that at the end of this Satanic unfolding we are presented with really only these innocence-experience alternatives: (1) pre-genital "innocence"—smooth-skinned, hairless, but excitable—the voluptuousness of childhood, or (2) the shocking damnations of experience—incest, wild passion, jealousy, forbidden knowledge, hidden treasure, to all of which the hero has been propelled by a kind of phallic mother (to use a relevant Freudian concept).

"Monk" Lewis's lascivious tale of the sins of a thirty-year-old Capuchin abbot can be viewed as a chamber of natural and supernatural horrors, in which a deep-dyed clerical sinner descends from a reputation for unmatched holiness and chastity through pride and the most degraded sensuality to shrieking death and damnation in the talons of Lucifer. But within this crude pattern there are threads of a finer and more delicate weaving, though no less poisonous. These threads let us try to trace. Ambrosio, the "hero," may be thought to initiate his course downward as he swells in raptures of pride at the enthusiasm he has generated in the crowds, for the author lets us know at once that this handsome and putatively holy man's voice can penetrate to the very depths of his female auditors' selves; but there is no doubt that it is the portrait of the Virgin, with her roses-and-lilies complexion and her white breast, which first arouses his libidinous desires. "Were I permitted to . . . press with my lips the treasures of that snowy bosom! Gracious god, should I then resist the temptation?" He transfers that emotion almost at once to the breast of Mathilda (a demon first disguised as a beautiful woman but now dressed in male clothes as a novice of the house) exposed in the moonlight to the abbot's hungry eyes, and, assimilating the charms of the Madonna to Mathilda in his feverish imagination, he soon yields body and soul to what looks to him like a living girl within the monastery walls. As she hardens into a libertine in both thought and action, the abbot tires of her and turns anew to innocence, particularly to the unspoiled delights of the fifteen-year-old maiden, Antonia, who seeks him out as her confessor. So powerful is Ambrosio's desire to overcome innocent resistance that he turns to black magic and to Lucifer himself, first for continuing visions of innocence and then to its rape amid charnel-house scenes of unspeakable horror. The murder of the virgin and her mother, the execration and damnation of the priest ensue, along with the revelation by Satan that the abbot's last relationship was with his own sister. Incest thus joins blasphemy and witchcraft, sororicide and matricide in a spectacular array of lurid evil. The sensibility that created such a story, which has soaked up venerable prejudices against the Roman church and displayed them with nauseating frankness, is of course acutely morbid; but it is morbid in a peculiar and revealing way. It endows virginal innocence with unconquerable fascination, for which the monk becomes willing to sacrifice his eternal well-being.

What Lewis has done in this once enormously popular novel is to inflate and pervert into horror the young bridegroom's dream of conquering nubile inexperience and possessing for life the fruit of the conquest. Denied to religious celibates, this route of libidinal release could become a nightmare of corrupted fancy and of corrupt deeds. Coleridge, expectedly, raged at the book and loathed its sensual horrors, but he was nevertheless capable of praising the author's imagination as "rich, powerful, and fervid." It might be instructive to try to conceive the emotions of Coleridge as he read this monument of the *Schauer-Romantik,* since he was himself at once a lover of virginal purity and a dreamer of lascivious dreams. But in considering these melodramatic fictions, it is not a simple and direct similarity with the Romantic spirit that I am seeking to emphasize but a disturbed and paradoxical affinity. It is true that Byron called *Vathek* his Bible, and that fact surely enforces traditional stereotypes about the poet. But far more memorable—and relevant to our theme—is his embodiment, in the Haidée-Juan episode of *Don Juan,* of an exquisite, though all too brief, moment of ebullient, natural, young, unspoiled love. The subjects of the following chapters, Keats, Wordsworth, and Blake, were all attracted by innocence and beauty, and the perversion of these qualities in Gothic romance must have seemed to be an ultimate betrayal. Just as we refer to ourselves as post-Freudian to indicate some kind of fall from earlier historical sexual innocence or simplicity, so we must view the Romantics as post-Gothic. However lofty the ideals of the early nineteenth-century poets may at times be, that sublimity must be seen as arising from imaginations that are irrevocably post-lapsarian. Blake's indictment of experience has in it much of the lurid audacity of Lewis's and Beckford's fictions. Wordsworth at least skirts incest, which for Shelley helps shape even his ideal view of the relationship between the sexes. And Keats yearned for the virginal somewhat as Ambrosio did and entered a hell of suffering that was not, however, primarily of his own making. The simple truth is that Romantic love, which often ended so tenderly, so comfortably, so conventionally, in Beulahs and in Grasmeres and Rydal Mounts, is nevertheless threatened by Gothic horror, disturbed by Gothic tension. But the Gothic never takes over completely, not even in the work of Byron. No one in the end goes to hell for love, which never seems to eventuate in permanent sexual disgust. One sign of this is that the great Romantics retain fresh and verdant some form of Eden.

Let Coleridge be our exemplar here. He saw sexuality as being present in the Golden Age, when between the sexes there was "just variety enough to permit and call for the gentle restlessness and final union of chaste love, and individual attachment." Such innocence he never wanted us to abandon. It possessed the "moral pleasurable feeling" which animates little children and maidens and also "those who in mature age preserve this sweet fragrance of vernal life, this Mother's Gift & so seldom kept Keepsake to her Child, as she sends him forth into the world—" (*Notebooks*, no. 3312). No wonder that Coleridge, reading *The Monk*, found that Lewis had extracted "pollution from the world of purity" and turned "the grace of God into wantonness."

The Epilogue of this book will consider briefly the relationship of its themes to major Continental philosophers of the period, but no student of the body in Romantic poetry should ignore the revealing contributions in prose of two minor English authors: the influential Richard Payne Knight and the typical and now unknown Thomas Little. The first is truly unconventional and modern in his orientation; the second is fresh, sensual, honest in his treatment of love but in the end, like many Romantics, a defender of basic, established sanctions and safeguards. Knight's treatise on Priapic worship often anticipates an important word, icon, or concept of Blake: his repeated use of *emanation* for sexual-mythic meanings is suggestive and anticipatory; and, with great relevance to our later discussion, he finds that the half-moon refers symbolically to female menses, the very symbol that Blake gave to his maternal, comforting, sexual Beulah. But direct influences are not here as important as Knight's Freudian habit of discovering phallic and vulvular symbolism in many pagan and even Christian myths and representations. In striking ways he sexualized the study of mythology, cultural anthropology, comparative religion, discovering both male and female physicality to be present in the generative rites of major forms of religious worship. Such sexualization constitutes an important precedent for Blake, Shelley, and Keats, though it is not fully relevant to Coleridge and Wordsworth. But even for these last, Knight's obsessive sexualism must have seemed to constitute a suggestive connection with Gothic fiction. For his attacks on Plato, his remarkably frank alternatives to the sexual escapism of Thomas Taylor's fleshless Neoplatonism, his phallic and generally sexual readings of venerable symbolism constitute dangerous but inescapable knowledge. To read Knight was to eat forbidden fruit, and man's imagination could never thereafter lose a post-lapsarian stain.

More than a generation later Thomas Little, not to be confused with the Anacreontic poet, Thomas Moore, who influenced Byron and who assumed this name as a pseudonym, directed his attention to the institution of sex as well as to sex itself. In a broad and unblushing survey, in which he quotes R.P. Knight (I, 249), Little stressed the importance of sexual pleasure for its own sake, in women as well as men, in many cultures and under many circumstances. He gave sexual pleasure this high accolade, that without it no parturition is possible and that there are therefore no accidental children, for children come into this world by the "spontaneous act" of a cooperating woman (II, 35). Little came to the optimistic conclusion that "we may experience perfect sexual enjoyment" in our human relations and that in marriage we can achieve "as constant a scene of delight as our being is susceptible of" (IV, 175). His optimism can be said to carry the whole eighteenth-century movement of sex and sensibility to the logical conclusion of fully available uxorial bliss. What was often only implicit earlier now becomes open, and Little opts for "intellectual improvement in the female" as the way to truly intersexual friendship and as "the surest . . . guarantee to society for a similar and corresponding advancement in the male" (IV, 165). Like the greater Romantics he finds the highest sanction for sexual love to lie in its omnipresence in nature. It is, in fact, for him "a law of nature" (III, 282).

But enlightened though he is regarding sexual pleasure and the importance of female satisfaction, Little is essentially conservative with regard to the institution of marriage and so recalls Wordsworth and Coleridge but not Shelley. The place for the sexual love so openly discussed in this treatise is marriage; and in marriage, as elsewhere, the man must lead since "he is born to command, the other to obey" (II, 31). Even in intercourse the superiority of the man must be respected, though it is probable that pleasure is "more extensive" in the woman than in the man (II, 35). But few, either liberal or conservative, have given so high a place to sexual pleasure as has Little — a pleasure "which affords the highest natural enjoyment mankind can experience on earth and is universally supposed to be the principle, in a state of essential purity, of the rewards of an hereafter" (I, vi-vii).

This introductory section on the body must, then, conclude with the thought that sexuality persists in both liberal and conversative opinion, in revolutionary turmoil and in domestic stability. There seems to be no room in Romantic sensibility for any kind of asceticism or sexual denial. In this respect our period is quite unlike any that has preceded — or indeed followed — it.

The Drive toward the Transcendental

Say, Muse! . . .
How Love and Sympathy, with potent charm,
Warm the cold heart, the lifted hand disarm;
Allure with pleasure, and alarm with pains,
And bind Society in golden chains.
                    Erasmus Darwin, *The Temple of Nature,* I, 3, 5–8

                              the overpowering light
Of that immortal shape was shadow'd o'er
By love; which, from his soft and flowing limbs,
And passion-parted lips, and keen, faint eyes,
Steamed forth like vaporous fire.
          Shelley, *Prometheus Unbound,* II.i. 71–75, *SPW.,* 228

Transcendence, which all the Romantics sought, is of course not the same as asceticism, a much narrower concept as it is a much more restrictive practice. In fact, inherent in almost any kind of intellectual formulation is a principle of transcendence, a linguistic and logical principle which is especially apparent when the subject concerns the material of any kind—the sensory, the physical, the terrestrial. Coleridge perceived this truth, as he perceived so much else: regarding materialism he said that as soon as it "becomes intelligible, it ceases to be materialism. In order to explain *thinking,* as a material phenomenon, it is necessary to refine matter into a mere modification of intelligence" (*Biographia,* I, 135–36, in *Coll. Works,* VII). One can conclude from such language that even to think about physical love is to start a movement toward its transcendence. Shelley, even when, somewhat sophistically and self-defensively, he opts for several love objects and forms (presumably three women are better than one), in effect applies the Coleridgean truth to our topic and extends love beyond the confines of the mind to the cosmos itself:

> Love is like understanding, that grows bright,
> Gazing on many truths; 'tis like thy light,
> Imagination! which from earth and sky,
> And from the depths of human fantasy,
> As from a thousand prisms and mirrors, fills
> The Universe with glorious beams, and kills Error.
>   [*Epipsychidion,* lines 162–68, *SPW.,* 415]

Such intellectual and imaginative transcendence of a reality like physical love resides in the very make and genius of poetry, if not of language itself.

I have dismissed asceticism per se as being outside the Romantics' ken, but does the transcendence that nearly always accompanies religion have any pertinence? Many Romantics, notably Novalis, Kleist, Coleridge, Chateaubriand, Lamartine, and, in his own way, Blake, were intensely fervent in religion, particularly in their moments of apocalyptic climax. Goethe's *Faust* ends with a Chorus Mysticus and with the pious feeling that communion with Christ and the Virgin is the cosmic core. The point is not that any of the aforementioned evaded human sexuality but that the Romantics had available to them all the usual religio-philosophical escapes from it or its debilitating and destructive energies. I have mentioned the Neoplatonist Thomas Taylor as at the opposite pole from the sexualizing imagination of R.P. Knight. Taylor read mythology as if it intended to blame sexual generation for everything evil in human life, and he thus blunted the sense of reality in the love and intercourse and even in the rapes and adulteries so prevalent among the Olympians: these "mean nothing more than a communication of divine energies." Stoicism now and then rears its head—we think of Wordsworth's turning toward duty, geometry, abstract thought, science, and Newton, although this strain in him, at least in his greatest period, by no means causes graces and smiles to cease together. The Romantics did not find congenial what appears in poets like Milton and Donne, whom they admired—an occasional snobbish rejection of sexuality as being too common, too democratic. Donne sang,

> Ends love in this, that my man,
> Can be as happy as I can; If he can
> Endure the short scorne of a Bridegroom's play?
> ["Loves Alchymie," lines 15–17]

And Raphael in *Paradise Lost*, in a passage that is, however, far from typical of Milton's glowing treatment of ideal sexuality, rebukes Adam for exalting sexuality:

> But if the sense of touch whereby mankind
> Is propagated seem such dear delight
> Beyond all other, think the same vouchsaf't
> To Cattel and each Beast.

> [VIII, 579–82]

Such an aristocratic and humanistic sense of superiority the Romantic psyche and ethos tended to reject.

A greater temptation than either religious etherealization of sex or impatience with its commonality is the drive toward regression and a turning away from adult consummations—either to childhood (even to childish sensuality) or to the generalized pan-corporal titillations of prepuberty. Such tendencies toward the sexually primitive would seem to be endemic in Romanticism, and one can see them present in forms of religious expression known to the period. The Herrnhuters, the Moravian followers of Count Zinzendorf, revived flagging devotion by celebrating "*Agapes* or Love-feasts" and embodied *das ewig Weibliche* in their religion by regarding the Holy Ghost as "the *eternal Wife of God,* the Mother of Christ." They tended to express love in childish diminutives that now and then anticipate *The Songs of Innocence,* though these earlier religious expressions can often be tasteless and sickening as Blake never is. Thus Christ the Lamb, the little Lamb, the little Jesus, is sometimes feminized into "Mamma Jesua." The wound in his "pretty little" side is called "the precious Hole"* and made a hiding-place for the faithful where they lie, eat, drink, sleep, and praise their cuddly Savior.

Leaders of intellectual, spiritual, and political movements, because they have wished total and unchallenged commitment, have often tended to be ascetic themselves or have proclaimed doctrines inimical to love and the family. Socrates, Plato, Jesus, Paul, Marx, though their movements have in time had to come to terms with human sexuality, initially derided, feared, or limited it. Many Romantics were of course the inheritors of what the critic and cleric Archibald Alison saw as perhaps the greatest gift of the eighteenth century (which he also regarded as superb in knowledge and virtue)—namely, its "humanity." Though not all would have agreed that this noble quality had "sprung from the fountain of the Gospel," these liberal and radical thinkers did have a strain of asceticism in them, and they frowned upon voluptuousness as softening the character or diverting psychic energies. For Mary Wollstonecraft sexual refinement and sophistication like that of the eighteenth century might sometimes make "the understanding the slave of the imagination" and even *sensibilité* could conceivably pamper the passions and "make women the prey of their [inflamed] senses." We now know *sensibility* to be a stronger word than was formerly realized (it could invoke the deepest and most searing passions known to man), but we must not swing so far away from traditional views of *sentiment* that we forget that sentimental-moral writers were often disposed to drown sexuality in delicately perfumed tears or to make love insistently innocent by a kind of unearthly *angélisme* that dissipated the physical. Even the Jacobin novel of purpose, which often tried to liberate love from parental tyranny and introduce the ideal of simple candor between the sexes, did not often dare to absorb the energies released by its own freedoms; and sexuality tended to remain tepid when it was not evaded altogether.

---

*I recall from my youth a prayer in a Swedish gospel-song, literally translated "Hide me deep in thy wounds." An American gospel song hails "The Precious Hiding Place."

20

Because these nobly reformatory or sentimental novels can be narrowly familial—the *mise en scène* enclosed in a world bounded by consanguinity—an aura of incest sometimes hangs over the relationships they portray.

Mrs. Inchbald's *A Simple Story* (1791) does present some love escapades, but the strong emotions of love-hate between the sexes—the locus of the genuine novelistic energies of this work—seem to arise from the relationship of guardian-ward early in the novel and of father-daughter later on. Although by her own account Inchbald's marriage was far from disastrous—she herself gave barometric readings of it that ranged from "happy" to "middling" to "unhappy"—her "median" assessment of the marriage is implied in her admission that the death of her mate left her "not unhappy." But for wedlock, she said, "friendship was too familiar, and love too precarious"—a view that may explain the sexual and marital evasions of this her best novel.

From all the above Jane Austen must of course be excepted. Her fictions possess what Juliet McMaster has justly described as "a kind of muted intensity that can be as moving as more overtly passionate novels." Such intensity bred in the fancy out of inexperience—a kind of "sumptuous destitution"—is not unknown in our literature; Swift (in his relations with Stella and Vanessa), Emily Dickinson, and Henry James seem also to possess and express it.

So much for evasions of sexuality. What can be said about the genuine transcendence of it? I have already suggested that one way to elevate the physical is to write or talk about it, to embody it in discourse or art. I have also suggested that religion could provide important ways to achieve exaltation. But the examples we have so far encountered seem rather to point to elimination, transformation, or denial than to anything more complex like the simultaneous elevation and retention of the original experience. Religion or religious-inspired visual art may help us to focus the problem. Raphael's *The Madonna of the Chair* (Plate VI) portrays a divine-human child and a woman exalted above all other women, but the artist here enforces only the purely human—a real mother and child in the enclosed spaces of maternal affection and childish dependency and joy. The same subjects in *The Sistine Madonna* (Plate VII) have by universal consent been thought to suggest the ethereal, the transcendent. By what means? Surely in part by the introduction of Saint Sixtus and Saint Barbara (possibly Saint Cecilia), ecclesiastical and hierarchical figures who stand for authority and belief. More importantly, by having the Madonna stand above terrestrial reality on a cloud, her posture and position suggesting the supernatural. But deeper than these iconic and positional suggestions are effects embedded in

PLATE VI. Raphael, *The Madonna of the Chair.*

22

PLATE VII. Raphael, *The Sistine Madonna.*

the art itself, in the aerial lightness of the bodies and the translucence that suffuses the Madonna's face. And yet, paradoxically, a fully recognizable mother and child remain central, and the supramundane suggestiveness in no way cancels or weakens their patently physical humanity. The faces of the holy pair and of the angels (the angelic pose and gaze may indeed be excessively humanized!) suggest palpable and universal human experience, a future experience of great dignity but also of pain. We observe a sense of portending tragedy but also of firm purpose, of a solemn mission to be accomplished through suffering. And it is precisely this rendition of profoundly human emotions in real people that gives the greatest depth and resonance to the painting, greater certainly than the more overt signs of transcendence. Indeed, the paradox lies less in the juxtaposition of the divine and the human than in the interpenetration of the two essences and in the persistence of the unmistakably earthly in sublimity itself.*

To get back to love and the Romantics, we should notice that when Coleridge in 1809 considers the shape of love, he separates it from outworn and conventional personifications and mythologies and places it where it belongs, in human reality; and thus here the only transcendence worth having must begin and end: "I like not your Cupids—Love exists wherever there is Goodness but it has no other Shape quite and exclusively its own—but that of Womanhood—and the modesty of Woman!" (Notebooks, no. 3561). Coleridge, a firmer believer in the transcendental than almost anyone else, nevertheless rejects purely decorative or conventional elevation, extends the quality to more than one or even several persons (Womanhood), specifies the ethical as a proper residence for love (Goodness), and isolates an individual trait as its sure sign (Modesty). We may today find other ingredients in love than Coleridge recognizes; the point is that at his loftiest he never deserted what belongs deeply to simple humanity.

To follow Coleridge and so attempt to see in the ideal the realities of life as we know and experience them daily may seem easy. But it is not. In the chapters that follow I shall attempt to display the complexities and explain the subtleties. Boswell, as worldly and realistic a critic of life and manners as ever was, distinguished two types of love, "the excruciating gloom of violent passion" and the more "general" kind, which is "gentle" and "pleasing." Subsequent discussion involving the

---

*An extremely striking and pertinent example of the extension of human reproductive sexuality into the sublime and the supernal, much to the improvement of the "higher" realm, is Hugo von Hofmannsthal's and Richard Strauss's Die Frau ohne Schatten, particularly in the Chicago and San Francisco productions of Frank Corsaro and Ronald Chase.

ideal will lead us often into Boswell's second kind of love, for the condition of tenderness and gentleness may well be the ultimate Romantic love-ideal. Edmund Burke, a much profounder thinker and perhaps a more complex personality than Boswell, also wished to emphasize ideal love in his political philosophy. He made such love the direct antithesis, not so much of fierce absorbing passion (though of course he feared shame and prostitution) as of abstract metaphysical speculation about love and manners, which he believed to combine unrealistic pedantry with the "coarsest sensuality." What did he oppose to such "unfashioned, indelicate, sour, gloomy, ferocious" attempts to create an abstractly conceived ideal "after the fashion of philosophers"? It was love that was gallant, fine, gentle, genteel, ornamental, gracious, mannerly. Reeking too much of the *ancien régime,* these qualities surely offended the nostrils of many Romantics. But as I have said, the positive ideal of gentleness and grace we shall find at the very heart of the Romantic love-ideal. And we shall see again and again how the great Romantics will anchor an idealized love in the family or in a closely related kind of community. They were truly the heirs of the eighteenth-century ideal of "esteem enlivened by desire" and of the Miltonic ideal of intersexual friendship in marriage. Samuel Johnson summarized that tradition in two complementary statements: "I do not pretend . . . to have discovered that life has any thing more to be desired than a prudent and virtuous marriage"; the duties of marriage are those of friendship "but exalted to a higher perfection." Such an ideal affected culture well below the level of Johnson himself or the Romantic poets. An anonymous pamphlet-poem of 1793, *Conjugal Friendship* (Worcester, 1793), partly literate, occasionally metrical, but in its own way touching, is a premarital meditation on the "nuptial union" that "shall take place / Between my friend and I." Its title page quotes the first passage from Johnson given above and expresses the ideal of a more perfect union than is usually known, "where Love and Friendship meet."

This humble poet walks on gouty poetic feet, but his ideal appears graphically in a genre of painting known as the conversation, group portraits of families or friends that are in the nature of things close to reality. As this genre continues its secular course, it exhibits signs of increasing intimacy and even the idealizing of intimacy. Such data appear if we pay attention to the following details, which only Ronald Paulson among critics has considered important: "who is next to whom, who is how far from or inclining toward or away from or touching whom, whose eyes meet, and who is standing or sitting next to what." With such concentration upon relationships we are able to see that in earlier conversations figures tend to be stiffly separated, even emotionally isolated from one another, but that physical rapport grows until in the later eighteenth century and the Romantic period real intimacy is achieved — and more.

A conversation by Gabriel Metsu, *Family of the Merchant Geelvinck* (Plate VIII), from the 1650s or 1660s should be allowed to set the earlier conventions: a heavy, assertive, proud, dominant father looks away from both his children and his wife; the maid holds the smaller child, while the mother merely helps steady a girl who sits on a table. The same "hierarchy of status and affection," to quote Ronald Paulson again, is present in James Maubert's *Edward Bathurst and Family* (1714/15), in which an infant does touch the mother's breast, though stiffly and awkwardly as the two turn away from each other, and in which the family members are rigidly separated; and in Hogarth's *The Fountaine Family* (1730–32), where the "program" of the piece keeps the women separate from the men, who, however, are warmly enough related to one another. Two canvases of Gainsborough are worth considering for what they suggest about the emotional temperature between the sexes. In the first, painted about 1764 and entitled *Mr. and Mrs. George Byam and their Eldest Daughter Selima,* the figures are elegantly clad and sophisticated in manner, but the couple seem detached from each other, though their faces are similar; and they seem also detached from what they see. The temperature is low, without any sign of rapture or even friendly rapport. In *William Hallett and his Wife Elizabeth* of 1785, also known as *The Morning Walk* (Plate IX), Gainsborough has given us a marriage portrait, called by John Hayes "surely the most perfect of the genre," a portrait in which he sees "the romance of young love." Both husband and wife are handsome, poised, aristocratic, self-possessed; and they are intent upon something in the scene. They are physically closer than Gainsborough's Mr. and Mrs. Byam, but one looks in vain here for rapture, physical attraction, or even sentiment. The picture is exquisite but elegantly cool, and the two examples I have chosen from Gainsborough both show attitudes typical of the earlier eighteenth century.

The bulk of the examples I have consulted in a fairly large literature devoted to the conversation seems to bear out the generalization made earlier, that family groupings before the late eighteenth and the early nineteenth century rarely portray warmth or even any kind of emotional sympathy, though mothers and children, often reflecting the traditional icon of Charity and her children, do move into intimacy fairly early. An important example would be Reynolds, *Lady Cockburn and her Children* (1775; National Gallery, London); and Rubens's representations of himself and his wife — if indeed they are conversations — would constitute a memorable exception.

PLATE VIII. Gabriel Metsu, *Patrizierfamilie (Family of the Merchant Geelvinck).*

PLATE IX. Thomas Gainsborough, *The Morning Walk*.

But in the Romantic period the conversation takes on greater warmth, either because of shared interest (as in music or art or a game or a contest) or because of obviously warmer familial ties. Of *Wir Drei* by Philipp Otto Runge (1804; destroyed in 1931), Hugh Honour says that what binds the artist-husband, his wife, and his brother together is the language of art, which Runge considered a "divine language"—"a secret Familiengespräch," the understanding of which created ties stronger than those of birth and marriage. But the very artistic arrangement permits one to ask if the marriage ties are not even stronger than those of family and art. A wifely arm encircles the husband's shoulder, and the couple's eyes are tenderer, more deeply engaged, and more fully expressive than those of the brother, who belongs in the circle of course but who leans the other way, presses his lips together, and looks out of the corner of his eyes in a whimsical detached way.

The other Romantic conversation I shall discuss, J.M.W. Turner's *Music Party, Petworth* of *c.* 1835 (Plate X), is fascinating because it suggests a greater unity among people than what one normally encounters earlier—a unity, incidentally, of a different kind. The painting therefore raises a question to which we shall return—what is the nature of Romantic unions between human beings? The room, like the human subjects, wears an air of aristocratic opulence. A man stands, a woman plays, another figure sits and looks at the performer. There is of course nothing original or unusual about this—musical conversations were common. But if we look more closely, we see another figure in the group who seems to be dissolving into white tulle or silk or even smoke, and we notice that many conventional and substantial items are melting into color, whiteness, or indeterminacy. Outlines blur, legs disappear, figures no longer stand upon a solid floor. But what are they dissolving into? Surely, palpable men and women are not becoming wraiths or ghosts before our eyes, partaking of a mystical experience. Or are they? It is possible that Turner is heightening into a kind of ecstasy the familiar warmth we have said was becoming increasingly characteristic of this genre. If so, a musical *soirée* is being made to suggest what is not easily representable on canvas, an intense kind of love fusion. More probably, Turner's scene represents the power of music to melt human divisions; but music, as we know from several traditional topoi, leads easily into love; and we may in fact here have a complexly mutating phantasmagoria of at least three of our themes—love, art, and transcendence. In any case, these shimmering but still fully social beings are a long way from the solid and stiffly separate persons who inhabit the conversations of Dutch and English art from the seventeenth through much of the eighteenth century.

PLATE X. Joseph M. W. Turner, *Music Party, Petworth.*

Thus painting, usually considered the closest of all the arts to reality, has also introduced a note of transcendence—first through a love and a sympathy within the family that seem to reveal physical warmth and spiritual rapport. But then in Turner come strong hints of even deeper fusions that do not, however, suggest the blindingly unmediated vision of the road to Damascus but the kind of union that can begin, if not end, in a musical salon. For even Turner has not allowed emotion to destroy the world or individual identity; he has only hinted at the possibility.

Mysteries of Eros in Coleridge, Shelley, and Wuthering Heights

> . . . *two great Sexes animate the World.*
>
> Milton, *Paradise Lost*, VIII, 151

> *When I love thee, what kind of thing is it that I love? Not the beauty*
> *of bodyes, not the order of tyme; not the cleerness of this light*
> *which our eyes are so glad to see; not the harmony of sweet tongues*
> *in Musique; not the fragrancy of flowres, and other unctuous and*
> *aromatical odours; not Manna, nor any thing of sweet and curious*
> *tast; not carnall creatures which may delightfully be imbraced by*
> *flesh and blood: They are not these thinges which I love in loving*
> *God. And yet I love a kind of* Light, *a kind of* voyce, *a kind of* odour,
> *a kind of* food, *and a kind of* imbracing, *when I love my God: the*
> light, *the* voyce, *the* odour, *the* food, *and the* imbracing *of my in-*
> *ward man, where that shines to my soule which is not circumscribed*
> *by any place; that sounds to myne eare which is not stolne and*
> *snatched away by tyme; that yieldeth smell which is not scattered*
> *by ayre; that savours in tast which is not consumed by eating; that*
> *remayns enjoyed which is not devoured by satiety; This is that which*
> *I love when I love my God.*
>
> Augustine, *Confessions*, X.vi.8ff, in an anonymous translation of 1620

In confronting the co-presence of the sexual body (about as clamant a physical reality as one can think of) with sublimity in love, we face a paradox as difficult to comprehend as the Christian doctrines of the incarnation and the resurrection of the body. It is baffling to logic and reason to try to understand precisely what "kind" of voice, smell, food, and embrace lingers on when Augustine loves his God in the inner man. Perhaps the best solution is to read and re-read Wordsworth's *Immortality Ode* and let its haunting hints of what "nature yet remembers" (line 132, *PW.*, IV, 283) of the supernal seize our spirits. But neither the Augustinian passage nor this poem, though they are closer to Romantic love-exaltation than are the body-evading Neoplatonists, quite unlocks the mystery, though they put us on the path. These works do not— indeed *could* not—point to the decisive presence in the Romantic spirit of the Enlightenment. The great poets of our period were raised not only on Rousseau and the masters of sensibility but on the *philosophes,* on the empiricism, the materialism, the associationism, even the religious Socinianism of the eighteenth century; and some of them made, at least for a time, some kind of intellectual commitment to rationalistic psychology, philosophy, or theology. What Wordsworth in the *Immortality Ode* called "sense and outward things" (line 143, *PW.,* IV, 283) tend to move all the way up into the "intense inane" of Shelley (*Prom. Unbound,* III.iv. 204)—a fact that makes Hindu and Neoplatonic formulae of transcendence irrelevant or at the most only partly relevant to the eroticized sublimity of the Romantics.

For Coleridge and Shelley it is the expositor's primary task to assert the importance of the body. Its necessary and desirable presence in love and thought each poet took great pains to celebrate. Sexuality in Coleridge is certainly complicated by neurotic, if not psychotic, tendencies in a personality inflamed by drugs and a perfervid imagination. A tortured man, he spent many nights on the rack, haunted by unspeakable horrors, by visions of castrating women and aggressive male relatives, by worries about potency and health, and by fears which the breast-imaginings and the recurring regressions to the comforts of childhood did not allay. He was clearly not the heartily, healthily sexual man that Dryden, Fielding, or Wordsworth seemed to be, though a closer look into each of these reveals unsuspected tortuosities. But the scholarship or criticism that stresses the narcissistic, the incestuous, the homoerotic, the perverse or that finds Coleridge to be profoundly repelled by normal sexuality and therefore always loathe to give the body its due has been much too dismissive. It also neglects to consider how he admired and desired normal heterosexual physicality, making it the very cornerstone of his thought about love and marriage. The sexuality embedded in Coleridge's greatest art insistently tugs at us—a fact that is quite amazing when one considers the sexual conflicts that tore and wore him and that would have led a man less committed to bodily love to silence or shame. I shall not rehearse here the many sexual suggestions in the great poems, except to go beyond most psychoanalytical critics and confess to finding that the fish and the nauseating sea-surfaces of *The Ancient Mariner* are phallic fish and sexual slime. But when "a spring of love gushed" (line 284, *CPWC.,* I, 198) from the Mariner's heart and began the process of spiritual cleansing, we are not to think that Coleridge intended that flow to wash away all human sexuality. Quite the contrary! In love, which is absolutely necessary to human life, growth, and integrity, Coleridge kept appetite and passion intact. "The greatest business of real unostentatious virtue is—not to eradicate any genuine instinct or appetite of human nature; but—to establish a concord and unity betwixt all parts of our nature. . . ." And the elements to be unified included "the concupiscent, vindictive, and *narcissine* part of our nature" (*Notebooks,* no. 2495). Coleridge believed that even the muscles pray (ibid.), that the body reveals the self—"She, she herself, and only she / Shone in her body visibly" (*Notebooks* no. 2441), and that there is "a sex in our souls." In a comment apparently addressed to his beloved Sara Hutchinson, he said: "Nay, I am no Angel; have no wings, no glory; but flesh & blood—the Lover's answer . . ." (*Notebooks,* no. 3406). This Sara he did not—indeed *could* not—marry, for he believed marriage to be indissoluble, including his own far from satisfactory one. And yet in marriage he located the apotheosis of love: "*Perfect* Friendship is only possible between Man and Wife: even as *there* is to be found the bitterest enmity" (*Coll. Letters,* IV, 904). But that perfection does not come if one conceives of conjugal sexuality grudgingly, as Paul did and as Augustine seems to have; one must regard it as an active virtue:

> yea, . . . the Pressure of the Husband's Hand or swelling chest on the bosom of the beloved Wife shall appear as strictly and truly virtuous, as *Actively* virtuous, as the turning away in the heat of passion from the Daughter of Lust or Harlotry. O best reward of Virtue! to feel pleasure made more pleasurable, in legs, knees, chests, arms, cheek . . . & yet to know that this pleasure so impleasured is making us more *good*. . . .
> [*Notebooks,* no. 2495]

Such intensity must be surely in part that of a deprived man dreaming of what might have been, but it is strong enough to enter both the carefully wrought poetry and the deeply meditated philosophy.

What, then, is transcendence of sexuality? We have already partly answered the question: it is the placing of physical desire in the nest, in the family, in an institution of safety, repose, tenderness, protection, where there are also subtle gradations and kinds of love, which give it a fostering and fulfilling environment. We must learn that sexuality is not only tamed and made tender in such an environment but is allowed full expression in different ways. Coleridge makes no sharp separation between kinds of love within the family, though there are of course profound differences in expression between them: "That beautiful feeling in the moral world, the brotherly and sisterly affections" are not harshly separated from "the conjugal affections," though they are divided and each kind is "as strong as any affection can be . . . ." Words often used of sexual love are extended to describe the "delightful intercourse between Father and child." The "beautiful gradations of attachment" in the family are educative and lead on to love of kin, neighbor, and countryman. But to get the force and nature of Coleridge's idealism we must note that the Christian paradox of body-soul co-existence is operating at full force and that the physical and spiritual interpenetrate. The affection of one sex to the other is made "strong" by sexual difference, which at the same time makes love "more tender, more graceful, more soothing, and conciliatory." Sexual difference is exactly what the term means, but at the same time it remains "perfectly pure, perfectly spiritual."

Such union of potential opposites would of course fly apart without clear priorities, and Coleridge gave primacy to love, not desire: "I desire because I love, and [I do] not Imagine that I love because I desire" (*Notebooks*, no. 3284). To achieve tenderness in love, Coleridge must abolish lust, separating it totally from tender affection. He himself had known what he called "loose women" between his nineteenth and twenty-second years, of whom he later (May 20, 1801) confessed that he could recall neither name nor face: "I remembered my vices, and the times thereof, but not their objects . . ." (*Coll. Letters*, II, 734). *Objects* these women had indeed become, and Coleridge apparently found that he had to banish from love an appetite that could be as reductive as that. In totally rejecting rather than refining lust, Coleridge differs from Pope, Wordsworth, and Freud, all of whom saw inevitable connections between lust and more exalted forms of affection. Coleridge is quite categorical in making his separation: "Lust can never be transubstantiated into Love." But he goes on to say that the *lusting* man can become a *"loving* Man" if and when he "deposits" his bestial nature and submits to "affections, Awe of Duty, and Sense of the Beautiful" (*Notebooks*, no. 2398).

"Awe of Duty" suggests Christian marriage and the institutional family, which we have already discussed and observed to be for Coleridge much more than a legally and religiously instituted society, since the family with its complex network of interacting members embodied different kinds of love that could be at once strong and tender, physical and spiritual. But the "Sense of the Beautiful" introduces art, for the Romantics one of the chief means of idealizing affection. Such idealization does not of course mean elimination of affection, and Coleridge turns away in disgust from the cool and loveless friendships of Swift's ideal horses, "In short, critics in general complain of the Yahoos; I complain of the Houyhnhnms." In Shakespeare and Milton, Coleridge found the precedents he was looking for: Shakespeare portrayed love and female character "with greater perfection than any other writer of the known world, perhaps with the exception of Milton in his delineation of Eve." The love of our first parents as portrayed in *Paradise Lost* Coleridge found to be "of the highest merit—not phantomatic, and yet removed from every thing degrading." To explain this union of real and ideal, of tender and rational, Coleridge invoked the full panoply of his critical ideals, so fully and memorably expressed in his *Biographia Literaria*. Adam and Eve together are like a great poem—"a union of opposites, a giving and receiving mutually of the permanent in either, a completion of each in the other."

Coleridge, a believing man, gave a religious dimension to love. How could he have escaped doing so? If love is like poetry in its uniting of contraries, both become logically related to incarnational Christianity. Thus the point of invoking Christianity was never to divorce love *from* life but to give it sanction *in* human life—in marriage, friendship, the family, and art. About the religious perspective I shall have more to say in the chapter on Wordsworth, when I compare his idea of love with his friend's. The important thing to see here is that Coleridgean religion idealizes love not by separating body and soul but uniting them integrally with great respect for each element in the union.

Shelley, the anti-Christian unbeliever, the uncompromising enemy of Christian marriage and the institutionalized family, the intense preacher of free love, did not of course seek any kind of religious sanction for the most exalted of his values; and sentimental love was exalted indeed. But this radical reformer of convention was himself often highly conventional in his tastes and practices—at least by modern standards. He hated birth control, libertinism, loveless sex, obscenity, rakishness, prostitution, and homosexuality, and he shuddered at the dark sides of adultery and seduction. Repelled by all these, he might have been expected also to have been repelled by any form of incest; but brother-sister sexuality he found to be only a crime of convention and on the positive side a highly poetical circumstance—for reasons that may appear when we discuss this topic in connection with Dorothy and William Wordsworth.

Fortunately, a competent modern scholar, Nathaniel Brown, has thoroughly demolished the idea of a "discarnate" Shelley, showing that the poet believed that romantic love existed "everywhere and always," that the sexual impulse is in and of itself an expression of love, that love is a permanent impulse of human nature. Expectedly Shelley's verse is viewed as "almost unsurpassed for its passionate evocation of the ecstasy of sexual consummation." But we must continue to inquire wherein, then, the obviously transcendental quality of Shelleyan poetic love truly lies, for he is not a sex mystic like D.H. Lawrence, who expected copulation itself to generate warmly and memorably its own lasting structures. Jerome McGann has said: "Eroticism, Shelley argues, is the imagination's last line of human resistance against what he elsewhere calls 'Anarchy': political despotism and moral righteousness on the one hand, and on the other selfishness, calculation, and social indifference." True. But more needs to be said about transcendence when the loving pair are alone, in close relationship, apart from society—and Professor Brown has said it. Platonically, Shelley believed in the partner as an antitype of the self, a mirror of one's own being. But, as we know from cultural history, even from Johnson and Boswell, the mirror is to be regarded not only as exactly reduplicating but also as idealizing reality. And the opposite sex—once the truly beautiful and appropriate nymph has been found—reflects back a cognate soul purged of selfishness and aggression, a soul whose lovely lineaments are drawn in the mind and usually only faintly shadowed in reality. To this idea as it appears also in Schlegel's *Lucinde* I shall return in discussing Keats's idea of sexual union.

In expressing the notion of soul upon soul, etymologically the *epipsychidion,* Shelley wears Neoplatonic garments, but he is actually closer to Plato (though of course in gender the kind of love is different) than to Plotinus or Thomas Taylor. There is no evasion of sexuality in Shelley's highest moments but an actual return to it—as Socrates in *The Symposium* returns to the earthly embrace for refreshment after stretching up dialectically to the eternal forms. This kind of paradoxical transcendence will appear clearly if we turn, not to the paeans *to* love in *Prometheus Unbound* (though these are positive and humane in their statements of sexual and amorous rapport) but to the embodiments *of* love in *The Witch of Atlas* and *Epipsychidion.*

The *Witch* is an intensification of general ideas about love, *Epipsychidion* an exaltation of a particular love. Love in the former is more basic than either nature or the imagination, with which the poem is also concerned. It unites mankind; civilizes satyrs, Pans, and Priapuses; calms wild nature; heals broken hearts; and consummates marriages. Yet, like all good ideas conceived of as ideas only, the two leading agents in the poem are conventionally sexless, each in a special way. The Hermaphrodite (Shelley loved the ancient androgynous marble statuary) is a favorably regarded being; and the poet, who believed love impossible without the elevation of woman to equal status with man, must have regarded his Hermaphroditus as an example of Platonic androgyny at its height, wherein the best of both sexes appears creatively intermingled. It includes the type and the antitype together. The Witch herself is also sexless but in quite another way—she ignores sexual monopoly and concentration; and that to many will seem like a deprivation of true sexuality. Flitting from flower to flower for honey, she expresses another Shelleyan ideal, that of a love that in Blake's words is "Lawless wingd & unconfind" ("How to know Love from Deceit," *E.,* 472). The *Witch* was written when Shelley was relatively free of particular entanglements. Mary had proved less than fulfilling, but he had not yet met Emilia Viviani. Without feverish emotion, free of social embarrassment, Shelley produced in this dazzling poem a freely willed, prankish, delightful but still intensely exalted expression of the love of love in its most typically Shelleyan essences. It is one form of Romantic idealization, brilliant but not typical.

The ideal of *Epipsychidion,* however, is rooted deep in personal experience and desire. Those involved in the actual love drama seemed to want to "Platonize" it out of immediate reality—or at least they could be thought of as temporarily yielding to that inclination. Emilia Viviani, a lovely girl from an aristocratic Tuscan family, who wrote often that her affection for Shelley was only a sisterly and spiritual experience, had written a little essay called "True Love," which she declared to be "an essence eternal, spiritual, pure, celestial." Mary Shelley called her husband's affair with Emilia "Shelley's Italian Platonics," and Shelley himself wrote to Claire Clairmont that his feelings for Emilia had no admixture of love and to Gisborne that his poem was a "mystery" and that he himself as poet does not deal in "real flesh and blood." The poem itself belies them all, including critics who have also remained steadfastly in the Empyraean. That is, the poem may or may not tell us what the life-relationship was like, but it surely records Shelley's strong imaginative understanding that such love ought to be sexual as well as spiritual. Neoplatonic ascent is indeed present; but if it is allowed to get in the way of perceiving the blazing, passionate carnality, the poem is badly misread and hopelessly distorted. For, as Carl Grabo has said, Shelley at his best can "spiritualize the flesh without denying it."

How can a critic convey that kind of achievement to the reader? That Shelley's total being was involved in the passion of the poem should be obvious to any experienced Shelleyan when the poet addresses the girl as "Spouse! Sister! Angel!" (line 130, *SPW.,* 414), thus invoking the full panoply of his erotic sensibility. She is a spiritually consanguineous being, his antitype. But if anything is clear it is that this soul out of his soul has thrown the poet into a fit of physical and imaginative excitement which he seeks to embody, somewhere, somehow, in a vital trope. His mind flashes out like the tongue of a serpent, or an insect, or like a tongue of flame, seeking to strike and consume. The process of exaltation is not orderly—indeed it is not a process at all. But it is brilliantly energetic as the poet reaches out for ecstasy. It is true that the more intense the passion becomes the more intent he seems on "killing the sense" (line 85, *SPW.,* 413), as particulars blur and flesh and blood quiver. But though the imagery ceases to be visually sharp, it remains sensual: Emilia continues to be a "mortal shape" (line 112), and warm and fresh fragrance falls from her light clothing and loose hair. The excitement mounts as the pair approach the isle of bliss, itself seen as "a naked bride / Glowing at once with love and loveliness" (lines 474–75), while the surrounding sea sparkles with sensual intensity. Love is alternately languid and burning, breaths intermix, bosom is pressed to bosom; and the souls burn as the wells of the psyche boil and bubble.

> The fountains of our deepest life, shall be
> Confused in Passion's golden purity.
>
> [lines 570–71]

At the end, as after all ecstasies, intensity relaxes: "I pant, I sink, I tremble, I expire!" (line 591)—not because the poetic speaker has lost faith in rapture but because he despairs that language can ever capture it. He seeks permanent, supernal forms, not to escape from passion but to prolong it in a "Burning, yet ever inconsumable" (line 579). Shelley was never closer to the passionate and immortal longings of Antony and Cleopatra or to the Keats of "Bright Star." In such vision how can one separate the ideal from the physical? The lovers unite and become one spirit, as the two of them fuse with their physical environment—with the

> overhanging day,
> The living soul of this Elysian isle,
> Conscious, inseparable, one.
>
> [lines 538–40]

A union of souls without doubt, but also "One passion in twin-hearts" (line 575).

Emily Brontë when portraying love between the first Cathy and Heathcliff in *Wuthering Heights* (1847) absorbed only the spiritual side of the Shelleyan fusion and so denuded it of some of its palpability. Joyce Carol Oates has said that this novel is "fiercely chaste, and none of its characters give any impression of being violated by a sexual idea"; but this comment should not be allowed to obscure the Shelleyan intensity of the union between Heathcliff and the first Cathy. Brought to the Heights as a substitute for her dead brother, the adopted Liverpool urchin and she live and love in a manner that suggests the incestuous— that suggestiveness itself being Shelleyan. But more pertinently recollective of the poet is the total blending of soul-essence that the two achieve: "I *am* Heathcliff"; "I *cannot* live *without* my soul!" (chapter 9). And to this love, which constitutes the major portion of the novel, Emily Brontë gives great existential power.

But how shall we judge it?

If we place alongside the Heathcliff-Cathy relationship the Freudian model, what does it look like? The pattern seems regressive. For the love begins in an idyllic childhood, binds both the lovers in an intimate identification with nature, torments each during a separation in the adult years, survives passionately the woman's marrying another, eventuates in the premature death of each, and points ahead to a reunion not in a Christian heaven but in some kind of sympathetic, all-engulfing nature. Perhaps Miss Oates's total denial of sexuality in the novel should be qualified: there does seem to be present in this union of spirit and mind a kind of pre-genital, diffused physicality that we see in bodies before they have matured into natural distinctiveness. In any case, Freud would surely have seen immaturity here, and the unbreakable union of two such beings he would have regarded as an example of natural mysticism, of that "oceanic" state, described in *Civilization and Its Discontents,* which does violence to the boundaries of a healthy ego and to the sense of reality by which we should order all our being and doing.

From a Christian point of view the affair is equally censurable. Heathcliff—at once an *über-unter Mensch,* a Byron, an Iago, a Satan, an Edmund, a Macbeth, a Richard III, a revenge or Gothic hero—is solipsistic and sadistic; but paradoxically he possesses these inward-driving qualities not all by himself but within the love-relationship or as a result of it. As J. Hillis Miller has said, "Heathcliff's cruelty toward others is a mode of relation to Cathy." Their union suggests incest early and adultery later, and it certainly has no issue, bears no spiritual fruit, possesses no ecstasy, and rises to no moral loftiness. And it drives relentlessly toward death. Passion there is, but it is the kind of passion— selfish, barren of normal sexual release, an unquiet anti-social craving— that the Christian writer Denis de Rougemont has censured in *Love in the Western World.*

I have used the word *existential* of it, and its power as *Existens* is indeed the only ground on which it can be admired. It has energy, power, superhuman *élan,* a yearning for wholeness; it asserts selfhood and being; it wills even death or rather life-in-death for the sake of ultimate union and integrity; and the compulsively driven couple go ungently into that Good Night.

But is it a *good* night? And can these primitive, dark, self-consuming energies be admirable? Apparently Emily Brontë did not, in the end, think so, for she created another Cathy, who did not have "her mother's predilection for the grave," to quote Miss Oates once more. And Heathcliff's successor Hareton is educated to read books and, along with his beloved, to reverse the antisocial obsessiveness of the earlier pair and enter into a fruitful marriage of mind and body. The new Thrushcross

Grange will be better than the old, which, with its shallow glitter, tended to produce "whey-faced" conformists somewhat smaller than life who fit into the conventional little boxes that Pete Seeger sings of. Thus finally Emily Brontë, though she may indeed reject the Gothic world we examined earlier in this chapter, does not reject the love portrayed in high Romanticism. For, as we have seen and shall see later on with greater clarity, at the very heart of Romantic idealizations stand sexuality and society, supported, directly or indirectly, by the Christian paradigm of the Word made flesh and animated by what Wordsworth called "vital feelings of delight" ("Three years she grew," *PW.*, II, 215).

2. JOHN KEATS
"The Chief Intensity"

Fair and foul I love together; . . .
Infant playing with a skull, . . .
Dancing music, music sad,
Both together, sane and mad.
Keats, "Welcome joy, and welcome sorrow," *CP.*,171

O, the sweetness of the pain!
Keats, "What can I do to drive away," *CP.*, 376

It is the contrariety of pleasure which most moves [Keats's] imagi-
nation.
Christopher Ricks, *Keats and Embarrassment* (1974), 145

Henry James said that "literature is an objective, a projected result; it is life that is the unconscious, the agitated, the struggling floundering cause." As a comment on some art in some periods, certainly that of James himself, Eliot, and other Modernist masters, the remark does not deserve Joyce Carol Oates's rebuke that the statement as dogma is "too blunt, too assured." But for Keats and indeed for all Romantic writers, James's separation of the fluid, uncertain cause from the objective and controlled effect is inapposite. Keats said of Shakespeare, with an equal and opposite privileging of life over work, that the dramatist "led a life of Allegory; his works are the comments on it —" (*LK.*, II, 67). The word *allegory,* with its hint of the older rhetorical separation of tenor and vehicle, will not do — the fusion of life and art in Romantic love-poetry requires something more Coleridgean and Donnean (like *interinanima-tion,* say). Such themes in particular bear the marks of life-pressures on them and reveal once again the impossibility of separating living impulse from shaped artistic form. Art both transcends and recalls "breathing human passion . . . / That leaves a heart high-sorrowful and cloy'd, / A burning forehead, and a parching tongue" (*Urn, CP., * 282). Essentially the same symptoms appear when Keats identifies a lock of bright hair as Milton's: "I feel my forehead hot and flush'd" — (*CP.*, 165). And more than once he referred to the mind producing poetry as being in a fever not unlike that of physical love; and of language itself he wrote, "I look upon phrases like a lover" (*LK.*, II, 139).

41

F.R. Leavis in our own century has said that "that exquisitely sure touch which refines and lightens Keats's voluptuousness cannot . . . go with spiritual vulgarity." Anyone who writes about physical sensations is always glad to be assured of ultimate refinement. But having been so assured, we cannot ignore this central fact: that Keats, in Matthew Arnold's language, was "abundantly and enchantingly sensuous." Many have failed to see or at least to emphasize and interpret the driving, torturing, shaping sexuality that is at the heart of the sensuousness. To Arnold's question whether Keats was "anything else" besides sensuous, our day has answered in glad affirmative. And if we tardily add to recent perceptions of Keatsian depth and dignity a revised emphasis upon sense, we should come closer to the truth than before. But of course the central questions raised in this study will still have to be answered: how is sexuality "etherealized," to use a favorite word of Keats, without being lost? What happens to it when it enters thought and poetic imagery? These questions can best be addressed if we follow, in chronological order, the unfolding of Keats's imagination in both the poetry and those profound and unfailingly vivacious extensions of the poetry, the letters, with their winning humanity and piercing pathos.

Bowered Bliss: "The Realm of Flora and Old Pan"
[1814–November, 1817]

> Light feet, dark violet eyes, and parted hair;
>   Soft dimpled hands, white neck, and creamy breast,
>   Are things on which the dazzled senses rest.
>   Keats, "Woman! when I behold thee," CP., 13

> Catch the white-handed nymphs in shady places,
> To woo sweet kisses from averted faces,—
> Play with their fingers, touch their shoulders white
> Into a pretty shrinking with a bite
> As hard as lips can make it.
>   Keats, Sleep and Poetry, lines 105–109, CP., 40

Keats said late in his pathetically brief life that "a man is like a magnet, he must have a repelling end" (LK., II, 240). One could say that also in his beginning was this particular kind of end, for the world of erotic faery that he created as his earliest poetic milieu has more than its share of the tasteless and cloying. Lawrence Lipking has taught us how crucial poetic beginnings are, and Christopher Ricks has made a good case for incorporating into life a sensitiveness to Keatsian sensations—"insights into life," he calls them, "which may be more accessible to a perceptive adolescent than to others." We may not like the heavily perfumed air of Keats's bower, but it is a world with its own kind of integrity and beauty. At the very least, to ignore it or cast it aside in disgust is to limit understanding of the seminal achievement present in Keats's earliest vision. The very vocabulary is important, for he sang "Of luxuries bright, milky, soft and rosy" (*I stood tip-toe,* line 28, *CP.,* 48), and the very word *luxury,* later refined but persistent throughout the poetry, is of importance, as are the qualities of whiteness, elegance, brightness, daintiness, gentleness, qualities shared by the landscape, the women in it, and the poetry describing it.

The sumptuous landscape with its leafy, flowery bowers owes much to the pictorial *poesie,* as they have been called, of Titian, Nicolas Poussin, and Claude Lorrain; and the nymphs and fairies of classical mythology are first mediated by Spenser, though without the earlier poet's firm civil, moral, and emblematic structures. The pearl-white and rose-red of the lady are Petrarchan colors, though here more vivid, palpable, and sensually insinuating than anything in those great but somewhat marmoreal and abstract Italian sonnets. One is tempted to call Keats's earliest creation a kind of living, organic tapestry, made of nerve and sinew with the flush of blood in it. Within this world we can see some progression—from poetry to painting as outside inspirations, for example—and there are other signs of dialectical movement: from the sexualized art-nature to human pathos, to the nobler life—a progress not entirely successful since we come back at once to the bowered bliss. Nor is it greatly significant that the appetite is aroused for darker, classical, Italian beauties in preference to the English, for this may be no more basic than a shift from Spenser to Titian. But there is at least one sign of real development, pregnant with promise: Keats seems to turn from the artificial world to the actual, the personal. Santayana has said that "half our standards come from our first masters, and the other half from our first loves," and he would be penetrating indeed who could determine the priorities here. Who knows now what adolescent prickings may have turned Keats to Spenser?

> If *you* think 'twas Philosophy that this did,
> I can't help thinking puberty assisted.
>
> [Byron, *Don Juan,* I.xciii]

In any case, one can only envy a culture and an education that could link the yearnings of puberty with the adventures of *The Faerie Queene.* But in reading the early poems chronologically, one can sense Keats's own age impinging on them, giving them a sense of relatedness to contemporary or slightly earlier literary-social phenomena. Robert Merry and the Della Cruscans, with their emphasis upon "sensate bosoms" and the rapture induced by white arms, had a generation earlier appealed to the urban classes—to milliners, maids, and city apprentices, not too far removed from Keats's own milieu of lower middle-class sensibility. Of course, the luscious and sentimental verse of Leigh Hunt, a friend, was a direct contemporary influence, linking Keats with liberalized if not radicalized expression. Thomas Moore's slightly earlier combination of the voluptuous and the tender achieved a more artful and tuneful melody than the very earliest Keats, but what Francis Jeffrey in the *Edinburgh Review* called "the perpetual kissing, and turning, and panting," from which he turned in disgust, is essentially grosser than anything in Keats, whose love of delicate innocence and purity remained an abiding predilection. Speaking of contemporary influences, we should not neglect society itself. It is probable that the change in female fashion, which now came suddenly to English women from France after the Peace of Amiens in 1814 and which favored the greater exposure of ankles and breasts while the muslin cloth clung to the figure, reached the sensational life of young John Keats.

From the erotic Eden of Keats's earliest verse, thus amply and complexly endowed, a vague poetic theory emerges; and one might have expected, perhaps even welcomed, a serpent form to creep out like a tempting phallic fantasy. Even the chaste Coleridge, at least in his *Notebooks,* followed the ancients and made a serpent in motion an emblem of poetic genius: "He varies his course yet still glides onwards—all lines of motion are his—all beautiful, & all propulsive—" (*Notebooks,* no. 609). Serpentine beauty Keats created later in his Lamia—after much harrowing experience of life and love. All the poet was ready for at this earliest stage was a mildly sexual epithalamion effect—not unimportant, to be sure, for the bower of married bliss appears crucially in the young man's sensibility:

> O for three words of honey, that I might
> Tell but one wonder of thy bridal night!
> [*I stood tip-toe,* lines 209–10, *CP.,* 52]

And in more general terms, in a brief pre-telling of the Endymion-Cynthia story, the story of a human shepherd in love with the immortal goddess of the moon, Keats clearly opts for a poetry of sexual fulfillment:

> The Poet wept at her so piteous fate,
> Wept that such beauty should be desolate:
> So in fine wrath some golden sounds he won,
> And gave meek Cynthia her Endymion.
> [Ibid., lines 201–204]

When we come to Keats's long, uneven, too often languid, but finally instructive poem on this theme, we encounter a sea-change. The sexualized landscape of the earlier poetry is still there — it resembles the beautifully languorous and sexually suggestive *Sleep of Endymion* by Girodet-Triosson, now in the Louvre (Plate XI), here rendered in verse richer than anything that Keats had written before, the eroticism having entered the poetic rhythms as well as the pictorialized vocabulary. Now plot supports picture, characters in movement replace nymphs in tapestry; and the dramatic placement of the older bower-like scenes reveals the experience of real life and the workings of an inquiring and unsatisfied spirit. It is to the revelations about sexual love in human experience, the central theme of the poem, that we now turn.

What do we learn? The very opening makes several telling points unexpected so soon after the earlier compulsions to inhabit a largely artificial bower:

> A thing of beauty is a joy forever:
> Its loveliness increases; it will never
> Pass into nothingness; but still will keep
> A bower quiet for us, and a sleep
> Full of sweet dreams, and health, and quiet breathing.
> Therefore, on every morrow, are we wreathing
> A flowery band to bind us to the earth.
>
> [*Endymion*, I, 1–7 CP., 65]

The passage seems to anticipate and answer the objections that have always been made to Keatsian eroticism, that it is feverish, languid, or remote. But here, though the bower is sexual, it is also quiet, healthy, sanely sweet, without burning forehead and parched tongue. Beauty lives with purely human joy, and the task of each day, though it is still concerned with creating the ordered and fragrant beauty of a wreath of flowers, is to use that "flowery band to bind us to the earth."

How can the earthly lover Endymion possibly achieve such an ideal? Not by settling for the attractive common sense of his sister Peona any more than by simply rejecting the "ardent listlessness" (I, 825, *CP.*, 84) of the earlier bower for a more transcendent, unearthly, and putatively permanent realm represented by Cynthia. And surely not by being seduced by the "curst magician" (III, 555), the regressive and lustful Circe, or even by yielding to the even more seductive attractions of the chaste Diana, another aspect of the moon, a goddess modest but finally life-denying, whose "white shoulders silvery and bare / Shew cold" in the "frozen purity of air" (IV, 586–87). Perhaps least of all by embracing a voluptuous death as the answer to our perplexities. On this last (and we should note the passage well, for on the matter of

PLATE XI. Anne-Louis Girodet-Trioson, *The Sleep of Endymion.*

death and the thirst for it Keats has been greatly misunderstood) the poem is categorical:

> We might embrace and die: voluptuous thought!
> Enlarge not to my hunger, or I'm caught
> In trammels of perverse deliciousness.
> No, no, that shall not be; thee will I bless,
> And bid a long adieu.
>
> [IV, 759–63]

Keats continually keeps a set of complex choices before the questing lover Endymion: he must reach high as poet, thinker, and lover, stretching himself above the earth though that aspiration itself risks embracing an illusion. At the same time, in order to avoid the "too thin breathing" (IV, 650) of Cynthia's "pure Elysium" (IV, 658), he must keep in touch with "this happy earth" (IV, 625), though this contact bears the risk of making him a "tranced vassal" to "the arbitrary queen of sense" (III, 459–60), Circe, or remaining a prisoner of his lovely, long-loved, but essentially unambitious sister Peona, who is not given to soaring and whom in one of his letters Keats used as a symbol of ordinary domestic, uxorial comfort (*LK.,* I, 175). Dramatically, the message is enforced by having Endymion end his quest by embracing in sexual love a beautiful, earthy, palpable human being, the Indian maiden, "the swan of Ganges" (IV, 465), who is then suddenly perceived in an apocalypse of vision as also being the radiantly golden Cynthia. So in the end the moon-goddess is incarnated and the shepherd-king of Latmos is, to use Keats's own word, "spiritualiz'd" (IV, 993)—spiritualized not through denial of sexual experience but through its full realization and transformation into what Keats will later call "the finer tone," the comparative of the adjective showing not abandonment but heightening and refinement.

The poet has thus moved decisively toward life and reality, where love is necessarily paradoxical, uniting contradictory elements into an uneasy union, volatile but potentially creative. For that kind of intensity Keats will have to use all the oxymorons for which he has become famous and of which we have a fair representation in *Endymion*: love is an "ardent listlessness" (I, 825), the "fairest joys give most unrest" (II, 366), the cry of the beloved is, "O bliss! O pain!" (II, 773); "Felicity" inevitably has an "abyss" (III, 176). Small wonder that the Keatsian poet will cry out, "Ah, what perplexity!" (IV, 447). Later we shall see how dangerous the love-serpent Lamia becomes when she tries to "unperplex" that perplexity.

In *Endymion,* Keats's long apprentice poem, he has forged on the smithy of his soul a mature view of sexual love as beautiful and real, as dangerously intense but also as capable of sustaining joy in love and art. To the exploration of such love as this Endymion and Cynthia go off together at the end. No longer can languid luxuries alone feed the mind ("Those lips, O slippery blisses"; those breasts, "tenderest, milky sovereignties" [II, 759–60]), though they live on in Keats's imagination, the most sensual of any within the compass of English poetic greatness.

This continuing presence of the lusciously sensual has of course been harshly judged. Byron called Keats's writing "*p-ss a bed* poetry," "the *Onanism* of Poetry," and the author a "miserable Self-polluter of the human Mind" (*Byron LJ.*, VII, 200, 217). John Jones has seen a "ghostly metasexual orgasm hanging over so much early Keats." William Walsh finds that for Keats being a poet meant being in a state of pleasure which "blends heightened and tingling sense experience with sensual and vaguely sexual relaxation." There is obviously much truth to such critical responses as these. A luxuriant sensuality was deeply implicated in the core of Keats's mind, not unlike Coleridge's, whose states of "pleasurable & balmy Quietness" (*Notebooks,* no. 1718) dreaming of breasts and of warm, lapping waters sustained a rich sensibility. But, to get back to Keats, we cannot forget the dangers of death and even of insanity that accompanied the younger poet's movement from his earliest sensual Eden to the paradoxical vision of love—truly a siege of contrary and conflicting agonies—which was achieved in *Endymion.* Nor should we fail to remember that, from the very first, love was brought into conflict with Keats's strenuous and demanding ambition to become a great poet. The struggle for fame, the wrestling with contemporaries and predecessors, undoubtedly added energetic morality to the luxuries of the senses and endowed Keats with what Lionel Trilling has called a "conscious desire to live life in the heroic mode."

"Solution Sweet": "Touch[ing] the Very Pulse of Fire"
(Late 1817 to late April, 1819)

> *Though one moment's pleasure*
> *In one moment flies,*
> *Though the passion's treasure*
> *In one moment dies;*
> *Yet it has not passed.*
> Keats, "Hither, hither, love," *CP.,* 61

You say you love, but with a voice
  Chaster than a nun's, who singeth
The soft vespers to herself
  While the chime-bell ringeth —
    O love me truly! . . .

O breathe a word or two of fire!
  Smile, as if those words should burn me,
Squeeze as lovers should — O kiss
  And in thy heart inurn me —
    O love me truly!

Keats, "You say you love," CP., 61

After having completed *Endymion* in late November of 1817 (Keats now having just become twenty-two years of age), a poem in which love was always threatening to become an illusion, he turned to life and reality with the most zestfully alert attention he was capable of. He sought for consolation against the wrongs of the world "within the pale of the World" (*LK.,* I, 179), and he consciously seemed to turn away from his "exquisite sense of the luxurious" toward "a love for Philosophy" (*LK.,* I, 271), a submission "to the command of great Nature," and a "continual drinking of Knowledge" (ibid.). Confessing to a thirst for knowledge that strikes us as resembling the consuming thirst of Samuel Johnson, he was happy that he did not give away his medical books when he abandoned surgery for poetry, and he revealed what many will find surprising in any Romantic poet other than Byron, a respect for the Enlightenment, for the "grand march of intellect" (*LK.,* I, 282) that made Wordsworth in some ways superior to Milton, though he fully perceived how Wordsworth also leads us into "dark passages" and imposes the "Burden of the Mystery," which the younger poet now wants eased (*LK,* I, 277). Such thinking led him to respect clarity and objectivity in art, "a more naked and grecian Manner" (*LK.,* I, 207), and in both men and women the qualities of probity and disinterestedness. These qualities can be opposed to sensation as such, and Keats rated them very highly: they "hold & grasp the tip top of any spiritual honours, that can be paid to any thing in this world —" (*LK.,* I, 205).

Reality for Keats had now come to include women (the women of real life and society, not merely of myth), the thought of marriage, and perhaps what Keats called "Venery" (*LK.,* I, 279), personal sexual experience. His beloved sister-in-law, Georgiana Wylie Keats, now in faraway Kentucky, he called "not only a Sister but a glorious human being" (*LK.,* I, 392). Jane Cox, the Anglo-Indian heiress and beauty, must have reminded him of the Indian maiden of *Endymion* (she was "not a Cleopatra; but . . . at least a Charmian. She has a rich eastern look; . . . she makes an impression the same as the Beauty of a Leopardess" [*LK.*, I, 395]); he was not in love with her, though she could haunt his nights "as a tune of Mozart's might do—" (ibid.). Finally Isabella Jones, a beautiful intellectual about his own age, who lived in tastefully furnished rooms, who liked to "collect" writers, and with whom Keats had a flirtation, seems not to have touched a libidinous or even a sentimental chord. All of the above taught him to be more relaxed and even self-masterful in the presence of women. They did not, however, resolve the extremely contradictory emotions which the opposite sex aroused in him—ranging from the highest feelings of friendship to those angrier, baser feelings that came out in what he called his "occasional rhodomontade in chitchat" (*LK.*, I, 325). In these outbursts denigrating women and marriage there is not much that is new—consult the tradition from antiquity through Shakespeare and Burton on faithless and deceitful women—and we do not need to bring the "rhodomontade" into the orbit of his poetic sensibility until we come to his very latest work.

All the women I have mentioned and also his dying brother Tom, whom Keats nursed, were powerful presences to him—"identities" (*LK.*, I, 392), as he called them, pressing on his ego and therefore on his poetry so powerfully that to get relief he had to flee to the abstractions (or the abstractness) of poetry. At about this time he developed his famous theory of Negative Capability—"that is when a man is capable of being in uncertainties, Mysteries, doubts, without any irritable reaching after fact & reason—" (*LK.*, I, 193). But, as we have seen, fact and reason are precisely what the post-*Endymion* poet *was* reaching after. So it may have been the potentially annihilating or otherwise threatening presences of real life and love that made negative capability absolutely necessary for "the poetical Character," which, he came to believe, "has no self—it is every thing and nothing—It has no . . . Identity . . ." (*LK.*, I, 386–87). The poetical character does continue to feel *gusto* and to experience *intensity,* both terms being prominent in Hazlitt's criticism and each used for strong feeling that excited the whole symphony of sense. These terms also possessed unmistakable sexual meaning, and we should not be surprised that the realistic Keats still called for "a Life of Sensations rather than of Thoughts!" (*LK.*, I, 185).

Some of these sensations Keats described as "high" (*LK.*, I, 277), and to all of them he applied the process of etherealization, *ethereal* being one of his favorite words. Certainly the imagination itself is the chief mediator of the ethereal, but that great faculty is also compounded of the "Heart's affections" (*LK.*, I, 184), and sexual longings. If we pursue further Keats's definition of imagination, we shall see that there is built into it the whole schema of the real-ideal which we analyzed in the first chapter. It possesses the passions which it can elevate to "essential Beauty" (ibid.). It is like Adam's dream — and Adam's awakening to the alluring, seductive, fully sexual Eve of *Paradise Lost*. The sexual component of the imagination is clear, but how does it idealize? What are its "empyreal reflection[s]" (*LK.*, I, 185)? Certainly Keats's idealizing imagination reaches out now and then toward immortality. He had received a liberal-Christian education at Clarke's academy, and his clerical friend Bailey did during this time testify that he possessed some kind of faith. A realm in which earthly happiness is repeated in "a finer tone" (ibid.) seems to have claimed an allegiance. But if anything is clear, it is that Keats was much more comfortable and persuasive when he heard the finer tone repeated on earth — when our sensations are reiterated, say, in the "delicious voice" of a singer with a beautiful face (ibid.). *Ethereal* Keats could apply to the effect of his beloved claret but also to poetic imagery produced by "the Sun the Moon the Stars, the Earth and its contents as materials to form greater things — that is to say ethereal things — —" (*LK.*, I, 143). No need to invoke a Christian heaven here or the Platonic world of forms. Keats is referring to the elevation a human poet can confer in what he calls "our most ethereal Musings on Earth" (*LK.*, I, 186). The "finer tone" could never sound without a sensational base; its "spiritual repetition" can "only befall those who delight in sensation" (*LK.*, I, 185). It is in this way that sexuality, the most powerful of our senses, enters into and endures in the imaginative life of humanity. Byron, too, had pleaded for the sensational life — "the great object of life is Sensation" (*Byron LJ.*, III, 109). But Keats's sensation was both more imaginative and erotic. Byron was content to see the sensational life as important only because it produced the feeling "that we exist — even though in pain" (ibid.). Keats went far beyond a sensationist affirmation of existence in seeing that sensation is etherealized in our highest humanity, that our moments of joy are suffused with sufferings: "Fair and foul I love together"; "O, the sweetness of the pain!" (*CP.*, 171, 376).

The post-*Endymion* realism and the revised philosophy of erotic sensation I have been commenting on bore poetic fruit, some of it strange, some of it over-ripe. *Isabella* and *Hyperion* I shall discuss in my summary account of Keats on death near the end of this chapter. Here I want to show how one of Keats's masterpieces, *The Eve of St. Agnes*, is exactly pertinent to the present discussion.

On 14 September 1817 Keats wrote to the Reynolds sisters that "I sincerely believe that Imogen is the finest Creature; . . . Yet I feel such a yearning towards Juliet . . . that I would rather follow her into Pandemonium than Imogen into Paradize-" (*LK.*, I, 157). Some have thought that Madeline is the object of Porphyro's voyeurism as Imogen is of Iachimo's, but I find Keats's scene to be an elevating revision of the Shakespearean mischief. And it is surely Juliet who became the Madeline of *The Eve of St. Agnes,* Keats's intensest presentation of the chief intensity. The idea of a poem on this subject was perhaps suggested by the elegant, intellectual Isabella Jones, to whom Keats had warmed and whom he had kissed; but the sexual consummation of the poem was surely a dream of union with Fanny Brawne, who has not yet entered our story but whom Keats already knew and loved (to her much of the concluding sections of this chapter will be devoted).

The modern metaphysical critics of Keats believe that Madeline's dream stands for imaginative vision and that Porphyro's entering that dream is the transcendence of reality by a pilgrim of eternity, whose presence in the bed of love is chiefly important because he thereby stores up experience for repetition in some kind of Platonic eternity. The blazing sensuality-become-sexuality of the poem belies that kind of idealization, as indeed does Keats's own comment and his own revision of the crucial stanza so that there could be no doubt that what he intended was unmistakable sexual consummation. He told Richard Woodhouse that Porphyro "acts all the acts of a bonâ fide husband, while [Madeline] fancies she is only playing the part of a Wife in a dream" (*LK.,* II, 163). He went on to say that "he shod despise a man who would be such an eunuch in sentiment as to leave a maid" like Madeline untouched (ibid.). Quite unlike the allegorizing critics are the more realistic commentators like Jack Stillinger, with whom I must also differ. He presents Porphyro as a seducer, Madeline as a hoodwinked victim, and Angela as a pander. Such a reading of the poem denies Keats his own carefully wrought passion and is therefore no less restrictive than that of high-minded abstractionists. Similarly, I cannot agree with those students of romantic irony who find the idealistic and the cynically realistic views equally persuasive, concluding that the poem leaves us in open-ended undecidability.

The poem is a masterpiece of the intensest eroticism, its intensity heightened, not obliterated, by the outside cold, frost, and sleet, by the aged servants, by the marmoreal dead who are as cold as the barely living aged, and by the hatred and blood-feud of the rival families. Porphyro's passion is indeed feverish, especially when set off by such artfully rendered frigidity. But then "Love's fev'rous citadel" (line 84) is not unlike the creating mind of the poet, as we shall see; the palpitatingly vivid descriptions of the viands, the casement, and the warm gules on

Madeline's breast are all of a piece — the sensuous becoming the sensual, intensifying by degrees into full sexual realization. Madeline, already erotically aroused in her fervid anticipations and also in her dream, is not unlike the dreaming Adam, whose awakening to the reality of a sexual partner Keats made a symbol of achieved imaginative beauty: like the first man she awakens to find her dream true.* And then she speaks in "voluptuous accents" (line 317) and fully partakes, though in the different manner of a renewed dream, in the sexual ecstasy. Surely many moderns will dislike the male-active/female-passive division of love labor in this climactic passage. But Keats, though he may have distinguished between *kinds* of sexual pleasure, refused to measure out the *degrees* of pleasure felt by each partner in mutual love: "who shall say between Man and Woman which is the most delighted?" (*LK.,* I, 232). I shall return in a moment to the climax, to the "Solution sweet" (line 322), but there is no reason at any point in the poem to doubt the palpability of the actors. Though they glide like phantoms to avoid arousing the sleepers, they are real flesh and blood — the wakeful bloodhound would scarcely have sniffed at ghosts; instead it recognizes a rightful owner. And I see no reason to doubt — though I do not want to suggest a bourgeois or Victorian nest — that Porphyro does indeed, as the poet says, have a home for her "o'er the southern moors," wherever *they* are, and that therefore the realized passion is premarital. Keats gladly provided all the honorable satisfactions his Saint Agnes virgin naturally required.

The lovers lived, loved, and fled ages ago, but this temporal remoteness does not chill their warm presences. It contrasts these lovers with those of Keats's nearly contemporaneous poem, "And what is love?" where "Antony resides in Brunswick Square" and "Cleopatra lives at Number Seven," modern love being "a doll dress'd up / For idleness to cosset, nurse, and dangle" (*CP.,* 220–21). One of the poet's great gifts is to bring the mythic "long ago" and "far away" into the living present as a permanent imaginative heritage. But *The Eve of Saint Agnes* is blazingly passionate and delightfully satisfying chiefly because Keats did not naturally take to unrelieved love and longing; such frustration was

---

*I do not wish to gloss over a difficulty here — Madeline at first finds the waking reality of Porphyro's presence colder than her dream and perhaps even threatening. But does this first reaction imply that the illusion of sleep is better than the reality she will now enjoy? Scarcely! She is a St. Agnes virgin, very young, inexperienced, and of course will be at first shocked by a physical intrusion upon her privacy. And she naturally requires assurances and pledges from a real lover. These she receives. With an exquisite and appropriate touch — we have seen that Keats loved innocence — he gives her a modest role in the ecstasy itself.

As though a tongueless nightingale should swell
Her throat in vain, and die, heart-stifled, in her dell.

[lines 206–207, CP., 235]

Keats delights in consummation. But having said all the above, I do not deny the piercing sense of loss that the grotesque concluding lines evoke with the "large coffin-worm" and the "palsy-twitch'd" face, meagre and deformed, of "Angela the old" (lines 375–76, CP., 239). The young lovers too will one day come to dust.

Milton's blushing angel Raphael in *Paradise Lost* celebrates heavenly copulation—"we enjoy / In eminence," a pleasure that is "Easier than Air with Air." Unlike angels, human beings do possess the "obstacle" of "membrane, joynt, or limb" (VIII, 623–26), and Madame de Staël's alleged comment on the human sexual situation may be relevant: "sensations delightful, positions grotesque." Human awkwardness may be one reason that there are in the vast literature of love few direct attempts, outside hard-core pornography, to describe the union of bodies. Where bodily details are not required, as in intellectual speculation, there is of course, especially in the Romantic period, abundant allusion to the love-embrace. As we shall see, Wordsworth in a literary context praised the union of sexually differentiated bodies as the great source of mental, including poetic, activity; and Coleridge, as we have seen, regarded sexual congress as the union of opposites, the blending of "the similar with the dissimilar," which is the "secret of all pure delight," including that of successful literary imagery. Therefore, even in contemplating a landscape, Coleridge emphasized that "Vision" is also "an *Appetite,*" demonstrating that even here intellectual effort for him resembled yearning of a sexual kind (*Notebooks,* no. 3767).

Actual literary representation presents problems that critical sentences do not, but a writer like Friedrich Schlegel, mentioned earlier in connection with Shelley's theory of the antitype, provided in *Lucinde* ("the best known and most popular novel to come out of the German Romantic movement") one of the fullest and most probing explorations of bodily union. Contributing to and influenced by the contemporary rehabilitation of Narcissus, this novel boldly applies the mirror image to intimacy—when the hero is literally close to and even in the heroine's body, his *membrum virile* "gross geworden" (47). At that moment, he sees in her a reflection of himself, not *gross* but refined, the sexual duplication endowing him with the delicacy and humanity which the woman has had all along. Such sensibility of the flesh—"die Empfindung des Fleisches" (58)—which the hero translates out of Diderot, led on to a sense of harmony that is religious and even mystical; and Hegel, Fichte, Schelling, to say nothing of Shelley, were able similarly

54

to elevate copulation, conceived of as a union of opposites, into a redemptive human ideal, similar to the spousal rites of man and God, of nature and humanity.

Keats, though he did say that Porphyro was "Beyond a mortal man impassion'd far" (line 316, *CP.*, 238), did not enlarge the union of his lovers into such philosophical orotundity. Nor does he achieve the love-union that Wagner does in *Tristan und Isolde*. I do not believe he would have been comfortable with the dissolving, "oceanic" imagery of the great *Liebestod* aria that concludes the opera. Isolde enters the waves of the sea, the breezes, the clouds, the blending odors, and drowns in a surging swell of water and melting sound. The "höchste Lust" is to sink "unbewuszt"—into the unconscious. What, then, did Keats do as a poet when the lovers attained the "chief intensity"? The lovers speak, and Porphyro's speech "flows / Into her burning ear" (*CP.*, 457), in the language of the revised stanza. Then, moving into metaphor, the lover melts into (in the revision "mingles with") the girl's dream

> as the rose
> Blendeth its odour with the violet,—
> Solution sweet
>
> [lines 320–22]

or, in the revision, less beautifully,

> as a rose
> Marrieth its odour to a violet.
> Still, still she dreams, . . .
>
> [*CP.*, 457]

We should observe that the revision metaphorically introduces marriage even at this feverish moment. As though reverting to the old belief, held in many Christian lands, that a true marriage took place when mutually pledged man and woman attained a consummation, Keats has Porphyro call Madeline his "lovely bride!" (line 334).

We do well not to allegorize, Platonize, "ironize," or sublimate the immediate reality of this union. Keats has etherealized it in his own way, which is the way of impressing passion on language and verbal form. It is the way of this poem's precursor, *Romeo and Juliet,* and it is the way of Coleridge, for whom "Love is a perfect desire of the whole being to be united to some thing or some being which is felt necessary to its perfection." In this poem Keats unites a bold lover with a passionate but coy and somewhat conventional maiden. The *Eve* celebrates what Blake called "the moment of desire" (*E.,* 50), but the implications go far beyond time and place not indeed to the defeat of death or to permanent escape from nightmare and evil but certainly to a more-than-momentary love that is absorbed, without loss of intensity, into death-defying poetry. This old-fashioned view—as I suggested above, a Shakespearean view of love, life, and art historically relevant to Keats—I do not wish to see deconstructed into an ambiguous irony.

The Great Odes and the "Fiery Gloom" of Fanny Brawne
[late April to July (?), 1819]

> O for a fiery gloom and thee, . . .
> Lead me to those feverous glooms,
> Sprite of Fire!
>
> Keats, "Song of Four Fairies," lines 72, 94–95,
> CP., 274–75

We have seen that in his post-*Endymion* period Keats turned to reality for ideas and inspiration, and we have also observed the tension that resulted from his dedication to poetry, which was often in conflict with the indissoluble identities the world imposed on him. Reality also produced Fanny Brawne, and no identity could possibly have been more pressing and inescapable than hers. Although he said later that he became her vassal a week after meeting her, he was able to establish a considerable emotional distance from her at first. "We have a little tiff now and then," he wrote, and he found her "beautiful and elegant, graceful, silly, fashionable and strange" (*LK.*, II, 8). She was short—a most important psycho-physical qualification for *his* comfort, for he must have suffered grievously from the fact that, fully grown, he stood only about three-quarters of an inch over five feet. He liked the modish hairstyles (often in the fashion of the Restoration) of the eighteen-year-old girl, thought her nostrils fine, her shape and movements graceful, and her arms good—auspicious details if we remember the white-armed, delicate nymphs of Keats's earliest bower. But on the negative side the twenty-three-year-old poet found Fanny's mouth "bad and good," her hands "badish," her feet only "tolerable" (*LK.*, II, 13). He considered her face to lack sentiment and her mind to lack ideas and information; and her behavior he regarded as giddy and even "monstrous" (ibid.). He was even impelled to call her a "Minx" (ibid.). I stress these quotidian, homely, and slightly compromising observations—and I have left out many (the close proximity of their living quarters, his disapproval of her desire to dance, their secret engagement, her later nursing of his tubercular body)—because Fanny Brawne was in many ways soberingly unlike the Romantic nymph. The *filles du feu*—the burning beauties loved by Gérard de Nerval, "pale as night" or "lovely as day," behind footlights on the stage or in the images of childhood, moving mistily in the "second life of dreams"—could live on in the French poet's mind for months, even years, without his bothering in the least about their reality or availability. Keats was far from indulging in that kind of nympholepsia. After *Endymion* he did not need to get into a Shelleyan barque and set out on a quest. It was not necessary, for Fanny was—or soon became—nearer than breathing and closer than hands and feet.

How could these admiring-censuring, playfully witty beginnings—Keats at first called his beloved Millamant (*LK.,* II, 36) after the witty heroine of Congreve's scintillating *Way of the World*—lead to the tyrannical passion that was to torture Keats beyond human endurance until the moment of his death. "Which anguish never ceasd," said the marvellously long-suffering, even saintly Joseph Severn, who attended Keats in Italy on his months-long death bed. How did the little, dancing, saucy, fashionably coiffured "Minx" become the poet's muse, the rich presence that lay behind and indeed sometimes became the *élan vital* of his greatest poetry? There are signs, even in the incipient moments of the relationship, that show why she was capable of being mythologized and so entering his poetry. For one thing, in the months after meeting her and coming to some kind of understanding about a mutual commitment, Keats went into a period of lassitude and passivity perhaps caused by the tubercle germ working within him. This state—which Keats called "a delightful sensation almost three degrees on this side of faintness" (*LK.,* II, 78)—we know to be the germinating time of his greatest poetry, the odes of May 1819. One of them, *The Ode to Indolence,* embodies precisely the personifications of love, ambition, and "my demon Poesy" (*Indolence,* line 30; *CP.,* 285), that the letters show appeared to him like figures on a Greek vase in his real-life state of languorous receptiveness. Fanny, whose pallor Keats commented on, may have been the possessor of the pale lips he kissed and of the "[fair] form / I floated with, about that melancholy storm" ("As Hermes once," lines 13–14, *CP.,* 246), both lips and form being present in the mid-April poems that must have arisen from the mid-April dream in which Fanny as Dante's Francesca unites with Keats as Dante's Paolo: "I floated about the whirling atmosphere . . . with a beautiful figure to whose lips mine were joined at it seem'd for an age—and in the midst of all this cold and darkness I was warm— . . ." (*LK.,* II, 91). The Shakespearean sonnet this dream became and from which I have quoted in no way rivals in artistic merit Blake's response to the same scene in Dante, his great painting and engraving entitled *The Circle of the Lustful* or *The Whirlwind of Lovers* (Plate XII); but Keats was then only weeks away from his own greatest poetic outpouring, in which, as in the inferno of germinat-

PLATE XII. William Blake, *Illustrations of Dante,* "The Circle of the Lustful" or "The Whirlwind of Lovers."

ing indolence, he was still imaginatively accompanied and sustained by Fanny Brawne.

Let us continue to look at the real-life Fanny for qualities that could be poetically viable. Keats had himself called her beautiful and was to insist upon her beauty again and again in his letters. Severn, a painter himself and a student of beauty, said she "strongly" resembled "the splendid figure (in a white dress) in Titian's picture of sacred & profane Love." If Keats had noticed that resemblance — or even if he had not, consciously — we can see how easily his beloved neighbor entered that embowered world of his fancy which Titian had earlier helped him to create. (Later Keats was to give to Fanny his copy of Spenser, another important inspirer of the bower of love in the earliest poems.) For the later poet, female beauty brought with it the whole panoply of sexual love, ardor, and devotion, as that shrewd psychologist, David Hume, said it would. Hume found love to be compounded of three different passions — the sensations of beauty, bodily desire or appetite, and good will. Love can begin with any one of these, "but the most common species of love is that which first arises from beauty, and afterwards diffuses itself into kindness and into the bodily appetite." Such was also the ordering of priorities in Keatsian love, and the primacy of beauty explains why he insisted so powerfully on the presence of that quality in Fanny, even apparently over her protests:

> Why may I not speak of your Beauty, since without that I could never have lov'd you — I cannot conceive of any beginning of such love as I have for you but Beauty. There may be a sort of love for which . . . I have the highest respect, and can admire it in others: but it has not the richness, the bloom, the full form, the enchantment of love after my own heart. So let me speak of you[r] Beauty, though to my own endangering.
>
> [*LK.,* II, 127]

These words, written on 8 July 1819, some two months after he had completed the great odes, express precisely the kind of love that suffuses them — a love that is explored and embodied in some of them but that is not attained in others. These poems, the best of them standing tall among the very highest verbal achievements in English, have been richly commented on, notably by Helen Vendler. In my analyses I shall stress the theme of my book, and the order I shall follow will reflect the presence in gradually increasing fullness of sexual love. Space will not permit more than a selective discussion, though each ode has a relevance, albeit sometimes indirect, to my topic.

From my present point of view the *Ode on a Grecian Urn* embodies a limited vision of love — the love frozen and unfulfilled, with the music unsensual and the bride (how unlike Madeline!) "still unravish'd" (line

1, *CP.*, 282) — placed, that is, somewhere between the altar and the bed. The status of the urn itself is repeated in that of the lovers on its surface frieze:

> More happy love! more happy, happy love!
>   For ever warm and still to be enjoy'd,
>   For ever panting, and for ever young;
> All breathing human passion far above,
>   That leaves a heart high-sorrowful and cloy'd,
>   A burning forehead, and a parching tongue.
>
> [lines 25–30]

The last words, especially in the context of Keats's own bodily sufferings, are moving, and the desire to escape such misery is an authentic human wish. But is it the desire of Keats's heart of hearts? Is it good — to go on further into the poem — to be teased out of thought either by an attic shape or by eternity? Can a "Cold Pastoral" (line 45) win over men and women of warm flesh and blood to a permanently satisfying insight? Is it indeed all we need to know on earth, that "Beauty is truth, truth beauty"? (line 49). Can this be the climactic condition to emerge from the vale of soul-making in real life when we have finally after much pain acquired "identities," each soul now "personally itself" (*LK.,* II, 102)? (Keats seems to have come to believe that the negative capability he once praised for having "no Identity" may after all be insufficient in the life- and art-struggle to achieve full maturity and inescapable individuality.)

I have interrogated the poem as Keats interrogated the Urn and have come to believe that No is the proper answer to all my questions. As one wedded to the belief that the matrix of poetry is life-experience more than antecedent language and form, I must take into full account the basically steady movement of Keats's spirit toward the acceptance of reality, however sharply paradoxical and incoherent that reality may in fact be. And so I tend to judge the Urn as less than life and consider the large generalizations about art that close the poem as being a serious qualification placed upon the transcendence of life expressed in earlier stanzas. And yet the poem as a whole does provide authentic interim expression on one level. Unconsummated, though deeply pledged, love exactly characterized the posture of affairs between Keats and Fanny Brawne when this poem was written. The kind of unfulfilled and unfulfilling foreplay — "For ever warm and still to be enjoy'd" (line 26) — is demonstrably an ingredient in pre-Romantic sensibility at least from Rousseau on, with its Canova-like delicate beauty of aroused but unappeased appetite, the beauty of sculptured *biscuit.* Though the temperature is warmer, the sonnet "Bright Star" does imagine an eternity of unfulfillment not unlike the imaginations aroused in Coleridge by the deeply loved but totally unavailable Sara Hutchinson. Fanny Brawne's "warm, white, lucent, million-pleasured breast" ("I cry your mercy," line 8; *CP.*, 374) is not exactly an urn, but it was at the moment as far from providing climactic satisfaction as the "still unravish'd bride of quietness": and Keats himself may indeed be the "Bold lover" who "never, never" can kiss "Though winning near the goal" (*Urn*, lines 1, 17–18). So truth—that is, authenticity to Keats's own individual experience and to at least one strain in collective European sensibility—can here be said to be beauty—the beauty of measured and resonant language. But still in the end it is not all that Keats—or we, for that matter —know or need to know on earth.

The *Ode on Melancholy* is highly relevant to our meditation on love, not chiefly because Fanny Brawne, perhaps with very little metaphorical distancing, is present in the second stanza as the mistress with "Peerless eyes and soft hands," raving and showing anger. The relevance lies in the fact that here Keats gives utterance to that central quality of sexual love we have observed as present in his sensibility from the very first: that it is deeply paradoxical and therefore inevitably oxymoronic in its literary expression. Beauty dies, Joy bids adieu, Pleasure aches and turns to poison; even more deeply—

> in the very temple of Delight
> Veil'd Melancholy has her sovran shrine.
> [lines 25–26, CP., 284]

Keats makes Melancholy a goddess but also a palpable female being, as Dürer had in his engraving and as Pope had in *Eloisa to Abelard*. She reveals herself only to one of the opposite sex

> whose strenuous tongue
> Can burst Joy's grape against his palate fine.
> [lines 27–28]

The orgasmic climax, troped by bursting ripe fruit, is uniquely and richly Keatsian, and the association of sex and sadness recalls the proverbial *post coitum triste*. More deeply, the moral-military metaphor suggested by *strenuous*, oddly but beautifully modifying *tongue*, hints that Christianity is appropriate* to the love-paradox: "Except a corn of wheat fall into the ground and die, it abideth alone: but if it die, it bringeth

---

*and so is Coleridge, who praised diffused sexuality ("the diffused or concentered Touch") but also accorded the specific sexual organs respect: "τα οργανα [sic; ta organa] *vere venerabilia*, an organ acting with what an intensity of personal Life/" (*Notebooks*, no. 1822). The Greek and Latin may be translated: the organs truly respect-worthy.

forth much fruit" (John 12:24). The ultimate result of the bursting of the sexual grape is of course poetry, but the shrine of Melancholy is a most important station on the way.

Helen Vendler in *The Odes of John Keats* dilutes her rich insight (that art and sexuality are integrated in the *Ode to Psyche,* a poem which she says unites the sexual Cupid and the spiritual Psyche in a "spiritualized eroticism" [64]), by her repeated insistence that in this poem, though in no other ode, Keats has "puritanically suppressed all the senses" (151) in favor of the working brain. The brain does indeed "work" (line 60, *CP.,* 277) in this poem as does the gardener fancy, and no one disputes that the ultimate subject of this poem is poetic creation. But the "rosy sanctuary" (line 59) of embryonic art is drenched with sexuality of a peculiarly Keatsian variety: thoughts grow with "pleasant pain" (line 52), the flowers breed, and "soft delight" (line 64) and "warm Love" (line 67) suggest the nest of intimacy. Perhaps the tendency of many commentators to unsensualize the poem and the poetic process it celebrates arises from the fact that Psyche has traditionally stood for the soul and that her mythic story has so often been presented as a spiritual and moral allegory only. But Keats was undoubtedly inspired by other interpretations of the legend—notably by the highly erotic frescoes, studied in engravings, of Giulio Romano in the Palazzo del Te, called by Fuseli "voluptuous reveries," but more importantly by the erotic-uxorial rendition of Raphael in the Farnesini Palace, Rome, whose "swelling and voluptuous grace" Hazlitt celebrated. It is with the purely erotic aspects of Cupid-Psyche that Keats began, in an early poem, his treatment of the myth:

> What Psyche felt, and Love, when their full lips
> First touch'd; what amorous, and fondling nips
> They gave each other's cheeks; with all their sighs,
> And how they kist each other's tremulous eyes.
> [*I stood tip-toe,* lines 143–46; *CP.,* 51]

In the ode Cupid and Psyche come together in a more beautifully poetic scene that is still highly erotic—more beautiful because more restrained and therefore even more deeply suggestive. "Their lips touch'd not" (line 17), but they are not like the *Urn*-lovers who never, never kiss. This pair will soon awaken and be "ready still past kisses to outnumber" (line 19). The calm sleep in Keats's bower is, shall we say, *inter*coital. But when Keats moves from the scene to the subject of the poetic mind, he does not go to allegory; he moves rather from Giulio to Raphael— that is, from the intensely erotic to the delicately but still warmly erotic-nuptial, thus finally recalling Porphyro's home for Madeline "o'er the southern moors." Poetry is imaged as wedded love, comfortable, bright, relaxed. In the "shadowy thought" (line 65) of the poet's working mind (recalling William Collins's "shad'wy Tribes of *Mind*") there is a welcoming home and hearth:

> A bright torch, and a casement ope at night
> To let the warm Love in!

[lines 66–67]

This is a complete reversal of the tradition of the escaping Cupid, who had immemorially been shown as fleeing out of a window as soon as his identity was discovered. Here Keats has created in the mind an open, receptive love, a "Merciful love that tantalizes not, / One-thoughted, never-wand'ring, guileless love," in which the palate of his mind will not lose its "gust" ("I cry your mercy," lines 2–3, *CP.*, 374; *LK.*, II, 279).

The *Ode to Psyche* fully fuses two themes often at sharp odds in Keats's mind and art, poetry and sexual love, in an artistic blending unequalled except in the ode, *To Autumn*, with which I shall conclude this chapter.

We have seen that Shelley's great love poem, *Epipsychidion*, also begins with a real woman and embodies the physical and intellectual excitement she arouses. Like Keats's elevation of love in *Psyche*, Shelley's intensification does not abandon the physical for the spiritual. But there resemblance ceases. Shelley seeks the soul within the soul, the soul in the other, as Schlegel did in *Lucinde*—the soul that matches his own. He seeks a consanguineous being, a union not with the opposite, the dissimilar—as Keats did in actuality and as Coleridge and Wordsworth did in theory—but with the profoundly similar, the "my sister, my spouse" of the Song of Songs.

The "Posthumous Life": The Passion according to John Keats
[Summer of 1819 to Keats's death, 23 February 1821]

> *Jailer. Come, sir, are you ready for death?*
> *Posthumus. Over-roasted rather; ready long ago.*
> Shakespeare, *Cymbeline*, V, iv

> *If she had a plague-spot on her, I could touch the infection: if she was in a burning fever, I could kiss her, and drink death as I have drank life from her lips.*
> Hazlitt, *Liber Amoris, Works*, ed. P.P. Howe, IX, 121

> *O what a misery it is to have an intellect in splints!*
> Keats to Mrs. Samuel Brawne, *LK*, II, 350

*I have an habitual feeling of my real life having passed, and that
I am leading a posthumous existence.*
Keats to Charles Brown, *LK.*, II, 359

How long will this posthumous life of mine last?
Keats to his doctor as reported by Severn, *LK.*, II, 378

On 25 July 1819 Keats wrote to Fanny Brawne, about seven months before his final illness was truly confirmed by a lung hemorrhage, "I have
two luxuries to brood over, your Loveliness and the hour of my death"
(*LK.*, II, 133). Had the death not been so tragically imminent, there is
hope that the loveliness might have been transmuted once again into
poetry, which would surely, however, have lacked the serenity of love
in the *Ode to Psyche*. As I have said, Fanny was a part of reality; that
reality was now tortured into a hideous paradox, each of whose elements
made insupportable demands—a paradox which precariously united
opposites in a tension more strenuous than any oxymoron in poetry
or art could possibly sustain.

Let us now examine both the heights and the depths. Keats's fidelity
to Fanny, which he tried hard to break, was in the summer of 1819 forged
into a band of steel. Her beauty still attracted him—"You dazzled me—
there is nothing in the world so bright and delicate" (*LK.*, II, 222), the
adjectives here being two of the most beloved in Keats's vocabulary of
love-address. He elevates his emotions into religion: "Love is my religion
—I could die for that—I could die for you. My Creed is love and you
are its only tenet—" (*LK.*, II, 223–24). But perhaps the most sublime
level of the relationship was reached when Fanny was truly felt to be
his muse, when she fed "the highest gust of [his] Life" (*LK.*, II, 279);
and that kind of etherealization was impossible except when poetry and
love united, as they surely did in Keats's imagination when the Porphyro
rose blended its odor with the Madeline violet.

The depths are as deep as the heights are high, and they get deeper
and darker as Keats "dissolves" (*LK.*, II, 223), to use the word he himself applied to his ebbing life. I shall not here go all the way into Keats's
hell, but I must point out that his jealous possessiveness, which Fanny
could not decently reciprocate at least at first, led to an unworthy striking back, to what he admitted was a "flint-worded" (*LK.*, II, 142) letter,
to bitterly disillusioned *humour noir* about men, women, marriage, sexuality, and birth, to fiercely infernal fire and ice unparalleled in the an-
nals of literary life in this period and not approached even by Hazlitt's
slavery to his unworthy urban nymph. Compared to Keats's, the burning tortures of Amfortas in Wagner's *Parsifal* were mild: the poet's wound

no narcotic could assuage, no Christian spear could heal. Readers of Keats's last letters, a climax of what the eighteenth century called the sublime of terror, will produce different nominations for the moment of the most exquisite torture. Clearly wanting to share intellectual pleasures with Fanny, who, as we now all agree, was fully capable of them, Keats marked the most beautiful passages in Spenser for her to read. Near that date, perhaps the next day, he wrote: "I am tormented day and night . . . I appeal to you by the blood of that Christ you believe in: Do not write to me if you have done anything this month which it would have pained me to have seen. . . . I cannot live without you, and not only you but *chaste you; virtuous you*" (*LK.*, II, 303–304). Perhaps that is surpassed by the cry to Charles Brown from Naples: "Oh, God! God! God! Every thing I have in my trunks that reminds me of her goes through me like a spear. . . . Oh, Brown, I have coals of fire in my breast" (*LK.*, II, 351–52). I myself, perhaps expectedly, find the most intense and harrowing sublimity of pain to be reached when Fanny as Keats's beloved muse seems to vanish from him into mist and darkness, no more available for either love or art: "The thought of leaving Miss Brawne is beyond every thing horrible—the sense of darkness coming over me—I eternally see her figure eternally vanishing" (*LK.*, II, 345). This is indeed searingly beautiful poetry arising spontaneously in the prose of a letter. But after that poetic cry, the sensations seem to have ceased being somapoetic, if I may say so, but became psychosomatic only. On his death bed in Italy the poet was able to dream of a reunion in England, but now—pathetically, tragically—the basic sensations of life necessary to poetic passion became purely lethal. He wrote from Rome (and we should note that he was being physically tortured in the stomach as well as in the lungs and the heart):

> There is one thought enough to kill me—I have been well, healthy, alert, &c, walking with her—and now the knowledge of contrast, feeling for light and shade, all that information (primitive sense) necessary for a poem are great enemies to the recovery of the stomach.
>
> [*LK.*, II, 360]

Keats had reached the deepest of the depths—not only poetic impotence but the indignity of feeling that what once inspired verse like that of *Psyche* or *Autumn* now only intensified the aches in the belly. But if we go back to the months before his strength began to ebb seriously—to the relatively safer upper circles of his inferno, as it were—we find him capable of producing the poetry of disillusionment about love and marriage, some of it very powerful indeed: in his one play *Otho the Great,* in his satiric *jeu d'esprit, The Jealousies,* also called *The Cap and Bells,* and in *Lamia*. The last-mentioned was written during July-September of 1819 after the great odes and in a period when Keats was desperately trying to establish himself financially and when troubles with Fanny (or more precisely with his own perceptions of Fanny) were at once darkening and illuminating the horizon. But at this time he was of course not yet on the rack of his "posthumous life," and he demonstrated that he was in full control of his medium, though one must concede that at the end of *Lamia* he seems to skimp his treatment of the cold philosophy and the colder philosopher at the end, an unfortunate poetic failure because posterity has taken over the censure of philosophic thought as being a central feature of the poet's mind when it is only a dramatic moment in an insufficiently developed conclusion. The portrayal of Lamia, the serpent woman, and of the romantic love she induces in a mortal being is, however, full, richly complex, and profoundly autobiographical.

Keats wanted his engagement to Fanny kept secret, and so it was — until almost the end. One of his deepest fears was that if brought into the public sphere of marriage — and also, with its disturbing demands, brought into his life as a poet — love, which he so much loved, would smoke away into airy nothingness. A related fear was that the circle of family and friends would continue to judge Fanny harshly and skeptically — a skepticism which might well smother poetry and love alike. One of Keats's intensest *cris du coeur* was his plea to Charles Brown from the boat en route to Italy to think well of Fanny: "You think she has many faults — but for my sake, think she has not one —" (*LK.*, II, 345). Both *Otho* and *Lamia* express many of the fears I have mentioned, and wedding banquets with family and friends present are unmitigated disasters leading to the death or disappearance of bride and bridegroom in murder, self-destruction, or an unexplained inability to survive.

How deeply Keats wanted life! But how deeply he feared what it might do to the hard-won structures of his cherished inner life and love! The greatest mischief of the enchanting witch in the poem is expressed in the following lines devoted to a description of her after she has entered life and in great anguish shed her gorgeous serpent form:

> A virgin purest lipp'd, yet in the lore
> Of love deep learned to the red heart's core:
> Not one hour old, yet of sciential brain
> To unperplex bliss from its neighbour pain;
> Define their pettish limits, and estrange
> Their points of contact, and swift counterchange.
> [Part I, lines 189–94, *CP.*, 346]

The wickedness of the witch lies less in her hypocritical virgin seeming than in her ability to tear apart what Keats after long intellectual struggle had discovered as a desirable and an inseparable union if a soul is to become an identity, if a personhood is to be created. The witch attacks the association of love and suffering, of pleasure and pain, and tried to explode from within one of the very firmest of Keats's paradoxical unions: "To unperplex bliss from its neighbour pain," to "estrange / Their points of contact." To do this would be to betray reality and create an incomplete or truncated existence that would wither and die. Thus to fracture the paradoxes Keats had so carefully nourished would be to deny negative capability, to short-circuit Keats's scheme of salvation through which an intelligence becomes a soul, to poison "the teat from which the Mind or intelligence sucks its identity," to blaspheme the "Minds Bible," the "Minds experience" (*LK.*, II, 103). What life hath joined together let no one, certainly not a beautiful temptress, put asunder!

In September 1819, about six months before the severe lung hemorrhage that he knew sealed his doom, Keats wrote the greatest and poetically the chastest of his odes, *To Autumn,* an affirmation of life and love. The mood of this poem, though autumnal in its own way, is not what one would expect of a Keats in love with death. But then such a Keats had not existed for very long, if at all, and I must now in a brief summary dispel what is still a common illusion about what has been called the poet's "instinct for non-being." It is of course true that in the *Nightingale* ode the poetic speaker declares himself "half in love with easeful Death" (line 52, *CP.*, 281); but such was never a permanent condition of Keats himself, though it admittedly has entered his poetry in "many a mused rhyme" (line 53). And Dr. Leavis is right to stress the "half" in the phrase "half in love," from which the poem turns quickly to the soaring immortal bird.

From the tortures of his posthumous life Keats would sometimes, though not often, call upon death to free his soul the nearest way, but such cries for relief from unbearable anguish can scarcely be regarded as erotic attachment to non-being. Apart from these cries there are moments in the letters and in some of the poems when he seems to be drawn to the luxury of death and its unconquerable quiet. Could it have been otherwise for one who saw his mother and brother die of tuberculosis even as he nursed them, who worked in a hospital as a dresser and surgeon, and who early in his own life felt the pre-sagings of fatal disease? Anyone who knew as much about *dying* as Keats did can be forgiven for now and then longing for *death.* But to think that that great and complex structure of emotions resting on physical enjoyment and including love was a house of death or even contained aesthetically attractive chambers of mortality is profoundly to misperceive Keats's art and spirit. It will simply not do to confuse Keats and the Wagner of *Tristan und Isolde*, where death and love, night and love, insinuate each other in virtually every breath of the music. Keatsian love did not drive inexorably toward death but toward life.

In *Isabella; or, The Pot of Basil* Keats made a beautiful and flourishing plant, smelling of a sweet balm, grow out of the green decay of a lover's rotting, slimy, decapitated head, kept in a pot by the grieving beloved. "'Twas love; cold,—dead indeed, but not dethroned" (line 400, *CP.*, 195). Not dethroned, to be sure, for the grieving maiden continued to love passionately. But surely not admired: Keats himself called the poem "mawkish" (*LK.*, II, 162). *La Belle Dame sans Merci*, strange and appealing, gives us a girl like the ones Keats had always loved in his fancy—long-haired, light-footed, wild-eyed; but the vision here turns out to be Circean (Keats had always feared and hated Circe). And the poet awakens to a reality that is pale, cold, autumnal, death-like. Keats is not in love with it; he is, rather, dismayed and tortured by it. In "Bright Star" the sexual emotions of the earlier copy by Charles Brown do indeed become "Half passionless" and in that condition "swoon on to death," but Keats abandoned that perverse type of feeling in his own later copy, in which death is thought of as desirable only if love and the eternity of the "sweet unrest" (line 12, *CP.*, 247) and of the "soft fall and swell" (line 11) of the beloved's bosom do indeed fail. It may have been grossly unrealistic of Keats to dream of such sensual immortality, but such moods do seize young men, who are, however, rarely able to transform them into permanent beauty.

Hyperion, an abandoned poem in Milton's manner, provides in its pre-Olympian beings a stern, strong, sculpturesque kind of sorrow that is "more beautiful than Beauty's self" (Book I, line 36, *CP*, 248). In some ways the Titans' gloomy grief is certainly a welcome relief from the excesses of the honeyed eroticism in Keats's earliest pre-*Endymion* poetry. But the poet's ideal of the later life-giving, love-breathing Olympian gods remains intact, however they may be modified as Apollo dies into life. Keats surely rejects the goddess Ops as an ultimate value, though she may make an interim contribution in the vale of soul-making. Her "pale cheeks," "forehead wan," "eye-brows thin and jet and hollow eyes" (Book II, lines 114–15, *CP.*, 259), do not finally win allegiance. The greater being, Moneta from the *Fall of Hyperion*—a vision of whom takes us deep into the Keatsian sublimity that follows the *via negativa*—is a version that goes far beyond the "lily and the snow" (Canto I, line 262; *CP.*, 367) of Petrarchism and earlier Keatsian sensuality. Here the poet confronts a face "bright blanch'd / By an immortal sickness which kills not" (I, 257–58), "deathwards progressing / To no death" (I, 260–61). Sublime though this is, Keats could not long have worshipped a Struldbrug, however elevated from Swiftian mire, and he abandoned this poem as he had its predecessor. The Titanic, pre-Olympian world is left a great architectural ruin, Miltonic in its dignity. It is grievous not to know what Keats, had he been vouchsafed productive life after his "posthumous existence," might have made of his own great sorrows. But there is no evidence that he became permanently attached to the flinty, death-like landscapes and the statuesque and infertile beings of Saturn's world.

In fact, the ode *To Autumn*, which follows the diasparactive imaginings we have been contemplating, is evidence to the contrary. As Helen Vendler says, Keats turns from Moneta, the chaste death goddess, "to the fruitful and maternal Ceres" (226). Continuing with Professor Vendler for a highly perceptive comment, we divine what the poet chose not to portray in *To Autumn*. "Many of Keats's verbs representing the actions of autumn are verbs having, if allowed to progress, a natural terminus: loading ends in overloading, bending ends in breaking, filling ends in overflowing, swelling ends in bursting, plumping ends in splitting" (247). But Keats does *not* allow these verbs of his so to progress, and in rejecting death and rottenness (which, as we have seen, he had earlier represented and turned away from in *Isabella*) he *does* present healthy garnering and certainly implies consumption of the goods of the earth and the entering of the ripe harvest into the continuing life-process. Keats in his last great poem, far from being in love with death, is amid growing tribulations invincibly in love with life.

Is he still in love with love? Unmistakably, though love is delicately and lightly expressed. In the last lines full-grown lambs bleat loudly, hedge-crickets sing, the red-breast whistles, "And gathering swallows twitter in the skies" (*CP.*, 361). Life, motion, action, flight! Sexuality also? Yes, truly—in the very cause of all this fruitfulness. The autumn season, personified as a woman and poetically painted in four very human poses and placed in scenes resembling actual rural life, is a "Close bosom-friend of the maturing sun" (line 2; Keats's old Olympian ideal, the god Apollo). Season and sun co-operate, "conspiring . . . how to load and bless / With fruit the vines" (lines 3–4); and to *conspire* etymologically means to breathe together, not inappropriate for bosom friends. A death is more than hinted at in the lovely sunset music, but it is surely Apollo dying daily into the continuing life of tomorrow's sunrise.

69

Where are the songs of spring? Ay, where are they?
Think not of them, thou hast thy music too,—
While barred clouds bloom the soft-dying day,
And touch the stubble-plains with rosy hue.

[lines 23–26]

The verb *bloom* adds vital warmth to this sunset collaboration, and the
"rosy hue" of the landscape is not the hectic of feverish death but of
life-giving love and reaping.

And so once more, and finally, we see how Keats at his best ethereal-
izes his sensations. He does so by terrestrializing, naturalizing, and then
poetizing the feelings that arise from the body.

And once again we must draw a contrast with Shelley. In the apocalyptic climax of *Prometheus Unbound,* another great poet of love unites
the moon and the earth in passionate love, but they are sister and brother.
From such Shelleyan love of similitude Keats had early turned away:
Endymion must separate from his sister, and he is able to unite with
the moon goddess only after she has become a dark, passionate, earthy
Indian maiden, sharply differentiated from her lover in virtually all
physical qualities. The two poets also diverge in the aim and scope of
their visions. Shelley, extending his to embrace all of humanity, recalls
in the words of Demogorgon the creative maternal bird of Genesis brood-
ing over chaos:

Love, from its awful throne of patient power
In the wise heart . . .
springs
And folds over the world its healing wings.
[*Prometheus Unbound,* IV, 557–58, 560–61, *SPW.,* 267]

Keats too reached out toward "the Sun the Moon the Stars, the Earth,
and its contents" in order to form "ethereal things" (*LK.,* I, 143). But,
as in this procession of planets, he tends to end on earth: it is enough.
His nature in *To Autumn* is the seasonal or daily nature of our common
life. And the love he celebrates, like Wordsworth's in the Lucy poems,
enters nature's diurnal round. The female and male are bosom friends
and collaborate to "fill all fruit with ripeness to the core" (line 6).

The poet who had begun by creating a blissful but artificial Spen-
serian and Titianesque bower for love has ended his quest in the energetic and self-fulfilling nature familiar to all of us. And his imagination
also found rest, though his own body and spirit never did, in "bedded
grass," "forest boughs," "dark-cluster'd trees," "streams, and birds, and
bees," in a flower garden with "buds, and bells, and stars without a

name," and above all in the adjoining casement "ope at night, / To let the warm Love in!" (*Psyche,* lines 15, 38, 54, 56, 61, 66–67 [*CP.,* 276–77]). Keats's chief intensity thus eventuates in a fruitful nature that has been comfortably domesticated. Nature is a garden, and the garden is opened on by a casemented window that implies a home.

3. WILLIAM WORDSWORTH
"Relationship and Love"

*To be at one with the otherness of nature is the arching comple-
ment to that other impulse, to be at one with the otherness of
people. The erotic life of nature, like that of other people, is both
warming and chastening to contemplate.*
Christoper Ricks, Keats and Embarrassment (1974), 210

*The poet, trusting to primary instincts, luxuriates among the
felicities of love and wine, . . . nor does he shrink from the com-
pany of the passion of love though immoderate —.*
Wordsworth, "A Letter to a Friend of Robert Burns"
(1816), Prose, III, 124

From love, for here
Do we begin and end, all grandeur comes,
All truth and beauty — from pervading love —
That gone, we are as dust.

Wordsworth, The Prelude (1805), XIII, 149–52

Having proclaimed in the *Prelude* of 1805 that love was the Alpha and
Omega of his song and the source of all value in life, Wordsworth pro-
ceeds to distinguish its four kinds. The first, the organic vitality of all
nature, manifested especially in the spring season, is followed by the
heart-touching, "tender ways" of the "lamb / And the lamb's mother"
(*Prel.,* 1805: XIII, 154–56, *Prel.,* 466). Since the poet is erecting a scale
of ascending values, even higher is the "green bower" of uxorial happiness, where with the "one who is [our] choice of all the world" we
"linger, lulled, and lost, and rapt away" (lines 156–60) — words surely bearing considerable sexual meaning. But highest of all is "a love that comes
into the heart / With awe and a diffusive sentiment" (lines 162–63). This
highest love, about which Wordsworth can be eloquent but certainly can
also be prolix and vague, is not my essential theme. I shall be concerned
rather with the human bower of love where man is "not alone" (line 157)
but can be "lulled, and lost, and rapt away."

Why should so many of Wordsworth's commentators have failed to
see such a central pre-occupation of the poet's best work? Hazlitt said,
"One would suppose, from the tenor of his subjects, that on this earth

72

there was neither marrying nor giving in marriage," and M.H. Abrams, who more luminously than any one else, has displayed the image of passionate marriage that is at the heart of the poet's high argument, nevertheless calls him an "ascetic" poet. Dr. Leavis has observed that "sex . . . is virtually absent from Wordsworth's poetry," and Carl Woodring thinks that "sexual passion has little space in his poetic canon; it is observed at some distance . . . it receives no open tribute." The weight of such authority is heavy, and it does indeed make it impossible to assert that Wordsworth was overtly, directly, or continuously a sexual poet.

Wordsworth the Man and Literary Theory

Is not the co-adunation of Feeling & Sensation the specific character of the sexual Pleasure: and that which renders this particular mode of bodily intercourse the apt outward Sign, Symbol, & sensuous Language of the union desired & commenced by the Souls of sincere Lovers?—

Coleridge, *Notebooks*, no. 3605, *f* 118

That the greatest of the Romantic poets was in fact sometimes a highly obsessed and more frequently a highly successful poet of physically based love, it is the purpose of this chapter to assert, and I am curious as to why the opinions cited above have become so pervasive, though they are by no means unanimous. They may go back to Shelley in this sense, that Wordsworth in personal manner and often in literary style seems to invite the charge that he was "a solemn and unsexual man," "a kind of moral eunuch," who "touched the hem of Nature's shift, / Felt faint —and never dared uplift / The closest, all-concealing tunic." No one but an unsympathetic satirist would have imagined Wordsworth engaged in so unseemly an act as Shelley describes, though, with considerable help from Wordsworth himself, we are tempted to be impish in some such way. Yet it is only fair to say that the few who knew him best in the days of his vigor as man and artist ever conceived of him as a male prude. That shrewd man of the world, Samuel Rogers, a writer not given to overstatement, remarked, "Few men knew *how* Wordsworth loves his friends"—the word *much* being clearly implied after *how*. Dorothy his sister was one of the few who knew, and she said that he had "a sort of violence of Affections . . . which demonstrates itself every moment of the Day when the objects of his affection are present with him" (*Letters Early*, 83). Coleridge said that "Wordsworth has the least femineity in his mind. He is *all* man"—a virility his tortured friend was capable of envying, sometimes morbidly and mischievously. And De

Quincey, who deplored the absence of sexuality from the poetry, thus described the poet's face, traditionally considered the *index mentis*.

> The nose, a little arched, and large; which, by the way . . . has always been accounted an unequivocal expression of animal appetites organically strong. And that expressed the simple truth: Wordsworth's intellectual passions were fervent and strong: but they rested upon a basis of preternatural animal sensibility diffused through *all* the animal passions (or appetites); and something of that will be found to hold of all poets who have been great by original force and power. . . .

De Quincey's last generalization may be as suspect as his "science" of physiognomy; but this is a verbal portrait drawn from the first-hand observation of a skillful writer, and its bluff and honest perception of sensuality must be trusted.

The strong animal appetites De Quincey saw mirrored in the poet's face are of course a natural endowment, and nature, traditionally thought to be Wordsworth's supreme subject, can scarcely be thought of as in itself ascetic or puritanical. But the most influential Wordsworthian critic of our day, Geoffrey Hartman, believes that Nature herself "weans" the poet's mind from "its early dependence on immediate sensuous stimuli," converting "the immediate or external into the quietly mediate, which then unfolds a new, less exhaustible source of life." It is the central view of this book, particularly of this chapter, that natural and bodily energy inspires and shapes the poetry of both tender familial affection and transcendental vision and that when it does not, the reason is not that nature is *exhaustible* but that the poet is *exhausted*. Wordsworth's own criticism, I believe, refutes Professor Hartman's thesis. If we consider carefully the famous statement, in the 1800 Preface to *Lyrical Ballads,* that poetry presents "emotion recollected in tranquility," we discover that what happens as we keep on recalling the original experience is not that the emotion but that the tranquility disappears and that an emotion kindred to the original stimulus "does itself actually exist in the mind" (*Prose,* I, 148).

Wordsworth's discursive writings on society and literature reveal the persisting presence not only of nature broadly conceived but of specifically sexual nature. His political philosophy, even as his conservatism grew upon him, rested firmly on the notion that the nation is, as he says in *The Convention of Cintra* of 1809, "a machine, or a vital organized body" (*Prose,* I, 225)—we shall later observe that in an important poem he calls his wife's attractive body a "machine" in this sense. The philosophy of society also rests on a belief in "the efficacy of principles and *passions* which are the *natural* birth-right of man" (*Prose,* I, 303, emphasis added). By passions Wordsworth says he means "the soul of sensibility in the heart of man," and he insists that such sensibility respects "the dignity and intensity of human desires" (*Prose*, I, 339). Both the dignity and the intensity—and we must take careful note of the point being made if we are to understand Wordsworthian transcendence—include the very lowest of the passions: "The higher mode of being does not exclude, but necessarily includes, the lower; the intellectual does not exclude, but necessarily includes, the sentient; the sentient, the animal; and the animal, the vital—to its lowest degrees" (*Prose*, I, 340). The lowest rung of this gradation we might call, in the words of "I grievéd for Buonaparté," "the stalk / True Power doth grow on" (*PW.*, III, 111).

Such a continuum is even more necessary to literary criticism, as we see in the famous Preface to *Lyrical Ballads* (1800), where the metaphors of the aroused senses keep animating the more abstract logocentrism. The real language of men is most available to poetry when it is in "a state of vivid *sensation*" (*Prose*, I, 118). The thinker-poet also possesses "a more than usual *organic* sensibility" (126). We associate ideas in "a state of *excitement*" (122, 124), and "the end of Poetry is to produce excitement in coexistence with an overbalance of *pleasure*" (146). The literary virtue called *pathos,* which goes back at least as far as Aristotle, Wordsworth brings into vital conjunction with his own comprehensive and realistic view of the animated world: our passions are "connected" with both "our moral feelings and *animal* sensations" (142), and "the pathetic participates of an *animal* sensation" (1815: *Prose*, III, 82). Can there be any doubt, if we concede power as well as meaning to discursive language, that the critic has actual human sexuality in mind and not merely the sense-data basic to empirical or associative psychology—a much-studied subject? Wordsworth himself seems to dispel doubt when he confronts "the pleasure which the mind derives from the perception of similitude in dissimilitude." He says:

> From this principle the direction of the *sexual* appetite, and all the *passions* connected with it take their origin: It is the life of our ordinary conversation; and upon the accuracy with which similitude in dissimilitude, and dissimilitude in similitude are perceived, depend our taste and our moral feelings.
>
> [*Prose,* I, 148: here and above, emphasis added]

This is the same continuum, including the lower appetites, that we observed as being functional in the political writings. Here the "accuracy" for which the critic pleads forces us to note that sexual appetites, however basic, are not themselves primary. What then is? Clearly, human differentiation, specifically sexual dissimilitude. This fact, as we have said earlier, clearly distinguishes Wordsworth, in theory at least, not from Coleridge and Keats but certainly from the pre-Romantic and Romantic love of delicate and only slightly differentiated bodies revealed in Canova's *Cupid and Psyche* and in Shelley's *The Witch of Atlas,* with its Hermaphroditus. Wordsworth may indeed be closely related to the earlier and more robust eighteenth-century traditions, expressed briefly and pungently by one of its leading medical men, George Cheyne, who in *An Essay of Health and Long Life* expressed the view that poets, writers, and artists — that *genus irritabile vatum* — possess livelier sensations than most and "generally excel in the *Animal* Faculty of Imagination."

To see the source of the pervasive pleasure Wordsworth finds in sexual differentiation and attraction does not, however, do full justice to what he is claiming here in these enlarging utterances. On one level he is asserting the importance of what Dylan Thomas called "the force that through the green fuse drives the flower" — a sexual force that pulsates in nature as energy and that continues to structure mental reality once the energetically sensuous details have become imaginative. But we must also see what the presence of sexuality has to do with the end-product itself, for Wordsworth is here speaking as a critic of poetry. If we translate Wordsworth's concern with difference in similarity and its obverse back to the ancient Latin formulae, *concordia discors* and *discordia concors,* and if we remember Samuel Johnson's brilliant uses of these terms, it becomes clear that Wordsworth is relating the union of sexual opposites in love to metaphor, simile, allegory, symbol, and variants of these — to the *wit* of good conversation and to the tropic structures of good literary ordering. Wordsworth, like Johnson before him, is transferring the ancient oxymorons, originally applied to the ultimately unifying struggles of love and chaos in the creation of nature, to the antithetical unions of wit and the imagination. We should note the impressive fact that Coleridge, who made the fusion of opposites the very essence of symbol, used that typically uncouth verbal construction of his, *coadunation,* for both the metaphoric structures of language and the union of "Feeling & Sensation" in "sexual Pleasure" (*Notebooks* no. 3605, *f* 118), an idea to which I shall advert in the Epilogue. Here I emphasize the unmistakably sexual parallel to the purely imaginative fusion:

> I cannot conceive of any thing more lovely, more divine, more deserving of our admiration, than that identification or co-adunation of the two lovers, Amatus Amata, in which each retains its individualizing contradistinguishing qualities, and yet *eminenter,* in a certain transcendent mode, acquires the virtues of the other — the rich tenderness, the woman elevation &c — the Sublime & the Beautiful —.
>
> [*Notebooks,* no. 4158]

Wordsworth, as we shall see at the very end of this chapter, was not comfortable with such Coleridgean fusion at its most transcendental, but his criticism shows him to be fully committed to a deep coincidence between sexual union and the creative reconciliations of imagination and art.

Sexuality is deeply pervasive in the thought of Wordsworth and his circle. What about his life and poetic practice?

Annette Vallon: Wordsworth's "Delirious Hour"

> *Farewel! those forms that, in thy noon-tide shade,*
> *Rest, near their little plots of wheaten glade;*
> *Those stedfast eyes, that beating breasts inspire*
> *To throw the 'sultry ray' of young Desire;*
> *Those lips, whose tides of fragrance come, and go,*
> *Accordant to the cheek's unquiet glow;*
> *Those shadowy breasts in love's soft light array'd,*
> *And rising, by the moon of passion sway'd.*
> *—Thy fragrant gales and lute-resounding streams,*
> *Breathe o'er the failing soul voluptuous dreams.*
>
> Wordsworth, *Descriptive Sketches* (1793),
> lines 149–57, PW., I, 50, 52

> *Tell all the Truth but tell it slant—*
> *Success in Circuit lies.*
>
> Emily Dickinson, *Complete Poems* (1963), no. 1129

> *What if we do discover that the greatness of poetry is grounded in animal passions? What if we do discover that the basis of all art is a certain measure of sensuality?*
>
> Herbert Read, *Wordsworth* (1930), 17

The ideas to be discussed in the remainder of this chapter are grouped around the three women in Wordsworth's life, his French mistress, his English wife, and his sister; but no one should conclude from this arrangement that I assume a simple equation between the life and the poetry. We shall soon see how complex that relationship is, how deeply sexuality can sometimes be buried, how skillfully disguised: as Herbert Read has said of Wordsworth, "By apostrophizing the mind, he hoped to conceal the significance of the body." The very complexities make it even more necessary for the critic to respect the ultimate source of Wordsworth's inspiration in nature and self and to disclose the currents flowing from the poet to his poetry.

In Wordsworth's poetic beginnings he sometimes strikingly anticipates himself and so reveals the essential integrity of his being. His early and energetic verses in *An Evening Walk*, published in 1793, about the rooster, in which I sense an undertow of sexuality, could be seen as a

foreshadowing of Wordsworth in his own ménage with Dorothy, Mary,
Sara:

> Sweetly ferocious, round his native walks,
> Gaz'd by his sister-wives, the monarch stalks; . . .
> Bright sparks his black and haggard eyeball hurls
> Afar, his tail he closes and unfurls.
>
> [lines 129–30, 133–34, *PW.*, I, 16]

Sometimes early Wordsworth even anticipates the voluptuousness of early
Keats: "Beating breasts" inspire the "'sultry ray' of young Desire"—

> Those shadowy breasts in love's soft light array'd,
> And rising, by the moon of passion sway'd.
>
> [*Descriptive Sketches,* 1793, lines 154–55, *PW.,* I, 50]

Wordsworth's walking tour of Switzerland in 1790 inspired these verses,
but he actually wrote them in 1792, perhaps not much before his de-
parture for England after his affair with Annette Vallon and some months
before the birth of his natural daughter, Caroline. He was then in the
firm grip of revolutionary sympathy, and, as was true of so many others
in this period, political passion was accompanied by sexual ardor. Indeed, the late F.W. Bateson believed that "Wordsworth would probably
not have become an active political revolutionary, if the barriers of his
passivity had not been previously overthrown by sexual passion. Beaupuy
[the young French officer who had guided Wordsworth into radical
thought] was only an effect, the cause was Annette."

The love of the French girl, four years his senior (he being twenty-
one), was known to Wordsworth's sister, wife, family—to his most intimate circle, where it caused neither grief nor jealousy, though it was
buried by his heirs deep in family secrecy until twentieth-century scholarship disclosed it. The facts are now well known and need not be re-
hearsed here, but a few summary observations need to be made to
younger students of the poetry. The passion between the young lovers
was strong and the desertion of the mother and child (owing to the outbreak of a long war) constituted a deep ravage of the poet's heart, from
which, however, he recovered without becoming embittered or morbid
about sexual experience.

It is undoubtedly true, as Emile Legouis saw, that Wordsworth's distress over leaving a mother and his own child in revolutionary, war-torn
France, now an enemy state, bore poetic fruit in the many "affecting
stories of seduced maidens, forsaken wives, or simply of wretched women
whose lives have been wrecked by the war." Every now and then in the
later poetry, even as late as Book VIII of the 1805 *Prelude,* there remain
pathetic moments that seem to recall desertion, with the details of course

altered. For example, a lone man comes out with a child to enjoy the sun and air; but then, as if to shield the child from these very elements, he bends over it: "He eyed it with unutterable love" (line 859, *Prel.,* 310). Does Caroline lurk behind the deeply loved child or Wordsworth's own paternal feeling behind the "unutterable love" the man is thought to display? But we are chiefly concerned with love between the sexes, not so much with the general psychological crisis that certainly affected the poetry of 1797 and 1798 and even later; and we must therefore inquire further into the poet's literary response to the passion that produced the child.

Much of that was buried on the Salisbury Plain, a wild and haunted setting. The poem, first named after the place and much later given the title *Guilt and Sorrow* (the title words must epitomize Wordsworth's own post-Annette melancholy), exists in three versions. The first (dating from 1793–94), within a year or so of his French experience, describes a Female Vagrant before she tells her sad story of desertion by her husband. (The true setting, is, I believe, France, but the poet sets the scene on Derwent water, psychologically as well as physically a place much nearer to his own heart):

> Like swans, twin swans, that when on the sweet brink
> Of Derwent's stream the south winds hardly blow,
> 'Mid Derwent's water-lillies swell and sink
> In union rose her sister breasts of snow,
> (Fair emblem of two lovers' hearts that know
> No separate impulse).
>
> [lines, 208–13, *Salisbury Plain,* 27–28]

The breasts here are sexually alluring, but they are not always so in Wordsworth, who in the intense, almost hysterical cries of "Her eyes are wild," has a mad girl say of her own abandoned breasts that they are now fiercely sucked by a hungry child as "fiendish faces, one, two, three, / Hung at my breast and pulled at me" (*PW.,* II, 108). But on Derwent water we have only the sweet sexual rise and fall of snowy breasts, those Keatsian delights, showing the wide range of his response to sexuality in this period. Even here, however, the sensual delights are followed by despair at the fleeting quality of love:

> And are ye spread ye glittering dews of youth
> For this,— that Frost may gall the tender flower
> In Joy's fair breast with more untimely tooth?
>
> [lines 217–19, *Salisbury Plain,* 28]

Finally Wordsworth turns to the plangent tale of the Vagrant's miserable life, heart-rending in its pathos.

Paradoxically, the passion in France that led to the sadness and pain associated with the Salisbury Plain had to await for more direct poetic telling until the Ninth Book of the 1805 *Prelude,* where in the relative calm of distance the "tragic tale" of Vaudracour and Julia, which Wordsworth heard in France, both resurrects and veils the story of Wordsworth and Annette. With some justification, though with considerable exaggeration, Matthew Arnold called this the very worst of Wordsworth's poetry. The story is indeed ineptly told and the plot is insufficiently motivated, but it has two moments worth observing by students of Wordsworthian love, one of grim intensity and one analytical of the very climax of the passion, of what Wordsworth calls the "delirious hour." As the story concludes—to confront the grimness first—Vaudracour ceases to be a manly, mature, hopeful lover and regresses to childhood. Julia thus has in effect two children, the infant offspring of the passion and the paternal wreck of that same passion. At one breast the child is suckled, while upon the other rests the "pale and melancholy face" (line 812, *Prel.,* 352) of the father. Whatever the causes in real life of the once passionate Vaudracour's regression to helpless abjectness—a hostile father, a hostile society, sexual guilt—Wordsworth's treatment of it could scarcely be less Keatsian; indeed, the scene could be viewed as a parody of "Bright Star," as a hideous inversion of dreaming forever upon love's fair ripening breast, to feel forever its soft fall and swell. Wordsworth would surely have penetrated to the potentially dangerous and illusory quality of Keats's poetic love in this utterance; but the evidence from the poetry before us is that he regarded Vaudracour's regression as more deeply dangerous and ignoble. Wordsworth's ultimate health in love did not come automatically or easily.

The analytical passage must be quoted in full, for it reveals Wordsworth contemplating a passionate moment surely like the one that produced his French daughter and presenting some ten years later the alternative he himself may then have faced:

>   whether through effect
> Of some delirious hour, or that the youth,
> Seeing so many bars betwixt himself
> And the dear haven where he wished to be
> In honorable wedlock with his love,
> Without a certain knowledge of his own
> Was inwardly prepared to turn aside
> From law and custom and entrust himself
> To Nature for a happy end of all,
> And thus abated of that pure reserve
> Congenial to his loyal heart, with which
> It would have pleased him to attend the steps

Of maiden so divinely beautiful,
I know not—but reluctantly must add
That Julia, yet without the name of wife,
Carried about her for a secret grief,
The promise of a mother.

[lines 596–612, *Prel.*, 342]

Wordsworth may be giving us a rare glimpse, though in fairly cool, structured, and not particularly inspired language, into his own ravished heart as he sees it from a decade's distance. The youth is naturally reserved and loyal, regarding himself as serving a divinely beautiful maiden; but the role strikes us as not a fully authentic one for the writer. He loved romance, as we shall see, and his eroticism is not untouched by Spenser. But can we take seriously his imagining himself, in revolutionary France with a pregnant and unwed mistress, as a *cavaliere servente*, as a gallant knight in a courtly tableau? But when he longs for "honorable wedlock," no one can doubt that the pull of that "dear haven" even the fervent young liberal felt as the very bias of his nature to the true magnetic North. Still, we must observe that he is not the least bit afraid to admit that the child came as a result of "delirious" passion, which he does not condemn. He even considers as a possible alternative rejecting law and custom and undertaking an entirely natural relationship. It is an eloquent fact that the poet of 1805, with his fully developed doctrine of nature, should imagine his own earlier self in crisis as being fully willing to abandon convention, throw himself upon nature for "a happy end," and put his deeds where his words are, trusting fully to the belief that "Nature never did betray / The heart that loved her" (*Tintern Abbey*, lines 122–23; *PW.*, II, 262). It is almost as exciting a moment as when Alexander Pope has his Eloisa passionately long for a life that is free, lawless, and unconfined. For our purposes now, the importance of the passage is that it shows that Wordsworthian nature unmistakably sanctions sexual passion and love and that to such shared vitality a man disappointed in the structures both of romance and of law and custom might gladly commit himself.

But however historically important or intellectually interesting, the passage does not come close to realizing—nor does anything else in the Wordsworthian *corpus*—what the poet calls distantly "the raptures of the pair" (IX, 635, *Prel.*, 344). Such emotions Wordsworth brushes aside as having been treated by more skillful poets than he. Why has he done such scant justice to the passionate ravage of his own heart's deep core? At first he *could* not fully confront it—the guilt and sorrow were too deep for measured words—and his poetic outlet came in the kindred subjects of desertion and suffering. He could apparently handle the results of passion but not the passion itself. And once his mind was healed, he turned to the healer, Dorothy, to neighborhood, to English nature loved since childhood. Treating such subjects in his own special way of indirect suggestiveness he restored the sensuous — and the sexual too — to his poetic personality.

It is about the persistence of sexual love that many critics and scholars need the correction that the balance of this chapter proposes to provide. Herbert Read, who deserves credit for seeing the enormous psychic importance of the affair with Annette, in which "animal passions, personal love, self-devotion — all had been engaged to their fullest degree," is nevertheless mistaken in believing that serenity was won only by the slow starvation of all such passion. If passion did not die, and I believe firmly that it did not, certainly guilt did; and F.R. Leavis is right when he says he finds in the poetry "no signs of morbid repression." H.J.C. Grierson has calculated that in the writings the ratio of the word *love* to *nature* is thirteen to eight. Where love is, sex in some form is sure to lurk, and Wordsworth could hardly have devoted so much poetic space to love and do so with such notable success and evident joy had his state been one of guilty fear. We must sharply distinguish his spirit from that of Felicia Hemans, whose works he owned and marked and who after early sexual disappointment apparently "drank in *soul*!" and indulged in a kind of "spirit-love" within the recesses of her "long-shut heart." Now no one can deny that there is evidence of suppression in Wordsworth's work. It could not have been accidental that, by William Empson's count, there are no examples in the 1805 *Prelude* of *sense* meaning sensuality, one of the commonest eighteenth-century meanings of that term. But *sup*pression — for reasons of modesty, taste, one's assessment of public preference, one's concern about one's friends or family or one's own personal image — is not to be confused with *re*pression. If Empson is right — and I think he is — that in Wordsworth "Sensation and Imagination interlock," it then must follow that sexuality remains an ever-present force even in transcendental moments, for there is simply no intellectually honest way of excluding it from so comprehensive a sensationism as Wordsworth's own literary and political criticism establishes.

Wordsworth was by his own admission moved by both conscious and unconscious pleasure. He also had experienced "the Nightmare Conscience" (*Borderers,* line 866, *PW.,* I, 162; the word *conscience* is of course closely related to *conscious*), and he was fully aware that the soul might sometimes receive "a shock of awful consciousness" (*Excursion, IV,* 1157, *PW.,* V, 145). In assessing the state of Wordsworth's mind, we can easily be misled by Freud and the moderns, who tend to be too fatalistic in making trauma permanent and who are not always historically just in understanding older vocabulary. From deep woundings Wordsworth seems always to have recovered, and by *unconscious* he seems to have referred not to guilty but rather to guiltless, worry-free, healing monitions. For one of the chief eighteenth-century and classical meanings of *conscious* and *conscius* was precisely guilty or criminal. And *unconscious* was therefore most likely to mean exactly the obverse.

When we come to the most fertile periods of Wordsworth's genius, sensuousness sparkles and crackles everywhere but sexuality is only implicitly present. Why such finding out of direction by indirection? In the words of Emily Dickinson, the poet may of course have wanted to

> Tell all the Truth but tell it slant—
> Success in Circuit lies.
> [*Complete Poems*, no. 1129]

If so, the reasons may lie in his own conscious choices, one of them undoubtedly the desire to be artistically effective. If there are other reasons for reserve and even chastity of utterance, these may emerge out of the contexts provided by his wife Mary and his sister Dorothy.

Mary Hutchinson Wordsworth: The Poet's "Dear Haven . . . in Honorable Wedlock"

Wisdom doth live with children round her knees.
Wordsworth, "I Grievéd for Buonaparté," *PW.*, III, 111

Life, I repeat, is energy of love
Divine or human.
Wordsworth, *The Excursion*, V, 1012–13, *PW.*, V, 185

I am giddy at the thought of seeing thee . . .
Wordsworth to Mary, 19 August 1810,
Love Letters, 90

Because what we may call the "Dorothy period" (from 1797 to 1802, the date of Wordsworth's marriage to the friend of his boyhood, Mary Hutchinson) was the most prolific in producing intense love-poetry and since I wish to reserve discussion of that verse to the climax of this chapter, I break chronology to consider now the poetry written during the early married life of the poet up to 1815, the year in which *Laodamia* was published. I do not analyze the very latest poetry because I take the usual path and regard it as being in such sad decline as to silence a commentator, particularly on the subject of love. I find that the mentality of the poet has now hardened into conventional stereotypes incapable of producing the fresh insights or utterances that invite contemplation. Declarations about love continue to be made, but they seem not to arise from the depths of the poet's being and strike one as utterly devoid of sexual energy. But that energy does continue to animate the poet and the poetry when as a husband he was enjoying and portraying "the gentle and domestic virtues of an affectionate heart."

We have seen how voluptuously Keats treated the legend of Cupid and Psyche. Wordsworth's response to it has hitherto been confined to a report of the painter Haydon, who believed that the poet was characterized by an "utter insensibility to . . . the beautiful frailties of passion," an indifference that seemingly became hostility when the two dropped in at Christie's one day and saw a statue of Cupid and Psyche: "Wordsworth's face reddened; he showed his teeth, and then said in a loud voice, 'THE DEV-V-VILS!'" It is unlikely that Wordsworth in 1820 was only feigning or mocking an emotion of sexual shock; but we now know that such an outburst was not characteristic of the period in his life we are now considering. On 7–9 May 1812, writing to Mary a love letter only recently published, the poet described at length Washington Allston's now lost painting of the mythic pair (*Love Letters,* 136–37). Though he found a little fault with the use of light in the execution, his pleasure was obviously intense. He dwelt upon the sensuality portrayed: he described without the least hint of disapproval the luminous naked flesh, the expression of enthusiastic love on the faces and in the attitudes of the subjects. In fact, given the context of sexual longing that these love letters provide, it is not impossible that he identified himself and Mary with the amorous couple on the canvas.

There was emotional, even physical, intensity at the heart of the intimate Wordsworth circle, what Thomas McFarland calls "the significant group." To some that small circle has seemed like a confinement. Keats, who admired its inmates, made this comment when the Wordsworths on one occasion departed from London: "I cant help thinking he has returned to his Shell—with his beautiful Wife and his enchanting Sister—" (*LK.,* I, 251). Surely to others the bland coziness of the *ménage* has been unattractive—with its provinciality, its self-flattering sense of safety and repose. It is true that union with Mary came during a time when Wordsworth was growing conservative in a truly English and rural manner so unlike the revolutionary, humanitarian, dawn-like enthusiasm for political change that accompanied the passion for Annette Vallon. But however much we may see repose in the Dove Cottage retreat, it will not do to look on it as sexless or passionless, the home of a frustrated man never able to recapture the first fine careless rapture of his Continental love.

Crabb Robinson once observed to Charles Lamb in 1816 (some fourteen years after Wordsworth's marriage) that "he never saw a man so happy in *three wives* as Mr. Wordsworth is"—the three being of course Mary, her sister Sara, beloved of Coleridge, and Dorothy, beloved of all. One is reminded of Samuel Richardson and his circle, which has been called a "harem," while the novelist's fantasies have been called polygamous. A closer parallel than the actual Richardson *ménage* is the situation of Sir Charles Grandison in Richardson's last novel, a parallel that suggests that there may be something in the English character, at least during the eighteenth century, that loved to multiply domestic presences, as though they were in a hall of mirrors. Sir Charles was passionately loved by at least four women. The one he finally married, Harriet Byron, a girl who possessed, besides the very highest principles, a fresh country skin, was not unlike Wordsworth's wife—also English, beautiful, radiant, kindly, gracious. Annette can perhaps be loosely assimilated to the Italian Catholic beauty, the Lady Clementina, who—and this is unlike anything we know about Annette—for a while lapsed into a serious love-melancholy. The fierce-tempered Olivia, a raven-haired beauty from Florence, and the fourteen-year-old ingénue Emily have no parallels at Grasmere or Rydal Mount. But the lively high-spirited, devoted sister Charlotte certainly does—in Dorothy, even though Charlotte married and Dorothy remained single all her life. The parallel is worth making because there is that in the domestic loves of the Wordsworths which looks very much like the culmination of the liberal, bourgeois, secular trend that Lawrence Stone has called "Affective Individualism" and to which I have applied the phrase "sex and sensibility." Coleridge, who saw limitations in Wordsworth's conception of love which I shall refer to at the end of this chapter, did concede that it "will do very well—it will suffice to make a good Husband—it may be even desirable (if the largest sum of easy & pleasurable sensations in this life be the right aim & end of human Wisdom) that we should have this, & no more— . . ." (*Coll. Letters*, III, 305).

Irvin Ehrenpreis has discriminated two contrasting views of familiarity in Wordsworth's own time. One is Sir Walter Scott's, that familiarity deadens sexual or romantic passion; the other, Jane Austen's, that neighborhood and close acquaintance quicken it. Wordsworth is decidedly a Janeite in this respect, for he believed that the poet, like the good and happy man he should also strive to be, must bring relationship and love into the very essence of being. As a civil man with a social conscience he hoped that by sending *Michael* and *The Brothers* to Charles James Fox he would alert the statesman and his Parliamentary colleagues to the threat that the spread of manufacturing and the new workhouses posed to what had been one of the great glories of the small independent proprietorship of English land—the domestic affections.

How they loved, these friends, neighbors, and relatives in the Lake Country! When, for example, Coleridge heard of the loss of Wordsworth's beloved son Thomas not long after the loss of a daughter, he wrote a letter (7 Dec. 1812) that ended: "Dear Mary! dear Dorothy! dearest Sara! . . . Again and again my dearest Wordsworth!!!" (*Coll. Letters*, III, 425). Such love in the extended group might not have existed had there not been at the very core of the nest a passionate, sexually fulfilling love between the husband and the wife. That kind of love did indeed exist, as we now know from the love letters of William and Mary, which came to light in 1977, which were kept a secret even from the significant group, but which the poet wanted preserved for posterity to see, all thirty-one, as a monument to his love.

These letters, written by both husband and wife after their first decade of marriage, yet possessing all the tender freshness of first love, must be among the most moving epistles of deep marital affection in English. Admittedly the genre is rare. One thinks back to the letters of Steele, but these of William and Mary totally lack the soft side that Dick expressed and also the contrasting hard, practical side provided by Prue. Here there is perfect frankness, trust, mutuality—and friendship. (The word is used more than once and the substance is unmistakably there.) An even higher perspective on the love is provided by the lovers themselves and conveyed by the repeated application by both of the word *blessed* to their relationship. Mary, like her namesake, bursts out in a Magnificat periodically: she has breathed William's name again and again to her children in his absence to give them some knowledge, conscious and unconscious, "how blessed, yea blessed above all human blessedness is their Mother.—" (*Love Letters*, 50).

Was there also passion? Indubitably, though it is expressed in the modest vocabulary characteristic of Wordsworth and his friends. Confessedly, some of the excitement arises from the fact that the passion is being written down. These letters bear out Foucault's point that language about sexual love may be even more important than the action itself, or Barthes's insight that the dialogue of lovers is more important than the very love, which of course could not have subsisted without articulation. Mary says it was "so new a thing to see the breathing of thy inmost heart upon paper that I was quite overpowered" (*Love Letters*, 46). She responds in kind: "now that I sit down to answer thee in the loneliness & depth of that love which unites us & which cannot be felt but by ourselves, I am so agitated & my eyes are so bedimmed that I scarcely know how to proceed—" (ibid.) I have already quoted

86

William's emphatically sexual description of a Cupid and Psyche painting. He also imagines an earlier scene when he and she might have been "fondly locked in each others arms" never to part (ibid., 61–62), and he confesses himself "giddy" (90) at the thought of seeing her. He calls Mary in almost Shelleyan terms his "love of loves" (59), he stresses the ardor of the love as much as its tenderness, he calls it a "passion" (62) which is "lively, gushing, thought-employing, spirit-stirring" (60). Such phrases, which Wordsworth might have used of nature or of his own poetry, recall not only Shelley but Keats, who also saw sexual love as employing the thought and stirring the spirit.

The mention of Keats reminds us of that poet's use of antecedent art to help produce as well as to reflect sensuality. Literary, though not pictorial, romance is also present in Wordsworth's love of woman; and he and Mary, like Keats and Fanny Brawne, together entered "the realm of Faery" (*Peter Bell,* line 101; *PW.,* II, 335) and "the hemisphere of magic fiction" (1805 *Prelude,* VI, 102–103; *Prel.,* 190), particularly "Spenser's Lay" (Dedication to *White Doe,* l. 5, *PW.,* III, 281). The beautiful but marmoreal poem, *The White Doe of Rylstone,* set in the chivalric past, is born in the bosom of Wordsworth's uxorial love. It now and then blushes a faint roseate hue but for the most part it is chastely and whitely cool. And one River Duddon sonnet, going back to "some far-distant time" (Number XXII, called "Tradition," *PW.* III, 255), though it is suffused with passion, warns in exquisite verse of the dangers that can attend the climax of sexual ravishment. *Laodamia,* a good if not great poem, is one of the substantial achievements of the Mary period. Wordsworth once compared himself to Mary, who was also "Nature's inmate" (1805 *Prelude,* XI, 213, *Prel.,* 426) and who had the gift of love. Like her, he said "I loved whate'er I saw, nor lightly loved / But fervently—" (ibid., lines 225–26; *Prel.,* 428). We are permitted to ask why in the poems just mentioned, the products of his love of Mary and with Mary of his love of Spenser and chivalry, he did not achieve fervency or even strive to cultivate passion. It is more than likely that the stoical control he prayed for after the shattering grief over the loss of his brother John in 1805 extended its restraints to "Tradition" and to the *White Doe*; and *Laodamia* will also have to be considered in connection with harrowing loss.

But first its story, a revision of one of Ovid's heroic epistles,* a product of what has been regarded as Wordsworth's period of discipline derived from the ancient Latin classics. Laodamia, a widow of the Tro-

---

*Heroides, no. XIII, "Laodamia to Protesilaus," is not an erotic poem which Wordsworth had to desexualize: far from being a Sappho, the ancient heroine is fairly close to what Wordsworth would want in a wife. On the other hand, the Romantic poet does not so much heighten as insert the stoicism, for there is none in the original.

jan war, prays to Jupiter to restore her slain lord, her bosom heaving in "impassioned" and "fervent love" as she prays. She is vouchsafed Protesilaus' return for three hours, and she then longs, "a second time" his bride, for "one nuptial kiss" on their "well-known couch" (lines 7, 11, 25, 63, 64, *PW.*, II, 267–69). At this rapturous desire, Jove frowns; and her husband, whose mead is now a spiritual love that is "equable and pure" (line 98, *PW.*, II, 270), rebukes her carnal passion, chiding her for not being strong in reason and self-government. In all versions of the poem Wordsworth seems to share Jove's and Protesilaus' and also the Parcae's preference for virtuous, disciplined, transcarnal affection.

What shall we make of such stoicism after the warm love letters? Surely Herbert Read is wrong either in condemning the poet for "manifest hypocrisy" in this poem or in seeing it as a late rebound from Wordsworth's own violent passion for Annette Vallon. From those flames Wordsworth had indeed emerged wounded, but he had been healed years ago. Can it be, as Donald H. Reiman has suggested, that after the loss of their two young children in the early summer and late autumn of 1812 something died in his feelings for Mary never to return and that the rebuke of the wife in the poem arises from his own sexual withering? In that interpretation the ghost in the poem admonishes Mary "to control her passion in the presence of a bodily lover who was yet only the ghost of his former self." This analysis is surely right in calling attention to the grief, for it was profound; but the suggestion of impotence, brilliantly ingenious though it is, strikes one as melodramatic and unproven, indeed unprovable.* Let no one, however, underestimate the suffering caused by the loss of the two sweet innocents (*Letters Middle*, 24, 32, 51), as Dorothy and also William called the children—first the loss of little Catherine and a few months later of Tom, the darling of Wordsworth's affection and his hope for the future, intellectually his most promising child. Families tied together in such intense affection have indeed given hostages to fortune! After the girl's death Mary remained in the deepest depression; after "my sweet little Thomas [was] no more" (50), William was once more "oppressed with sorrow and distracted with anxiety" (53); and one suspects that Wordsworth's language reveals only the tip of the iceberg. In fact, he wrote almost a month later: "we have suffered as much anguish as it is possible to undergo in a like case" (56); and a few weeks later still he referred to "my present depression of mind" (66). He was said by Dorothy to have aged ten years

*We should note that there was worry about a pregnancy for Mary after her great grief, showing that sexual relations were thought to have continued at least until some time before 6 April 1813. See *Letters Middle*, III, 89.

in a few weeks, while Mary remained "greatly shattered" (85) for months, and there was even some despair over her recovery. The grief of both husband and wife bordered on impiety as well as madness, for Wordsworth seemed to have felt an inability to pray. So the ghost who warns in *Laodamia* against "rebellious passion" and "the tumult of the soul" and who recommends that human beings "meekly mourn" in "fervent, not ungovernable, love," in "transports moderate," may have found fit audience in *both* the poet himself and his wife (lines 74–77, *PW.*, II, 269).

It is surely not sexual love per se that is rebuked in *Laodamia*. We must remember that the embraces the husband now discourages are between a living human being and a ghost. Laodamia is tragically deluded when she cries out, "No Spectre greets me," for that is exactly what she encounters—a "vain Shadow," now "no blooming Hero" (lines 61, 62, *PW.*, II, 269). She has mistaken the dead for the living in a mischievously misplaced affection that has, to be sure, arisen from recollections of physical bliss and deep love but that should by no means be necessarily identified with sexuality in and of itself. Laodamia's sin is therefore far from what Defoe called "conjugal lewdness" or from the excessive passion in the married state that the present Pope, following a long tradition, has recently so sternly condemned. Her sin lies in mistaking the dead for the living, in a refusal to accept the limits of mortality, in a failure to acquiesce in the inescapable law that death follows life.

Portions of that overly long, occasionally pompous or flaccid, but often majestic poem, *The Excursion,* come from the very experiences we have seen to underlie *Laodamia*. Some passages in its first book, going back as far as 1797, do breathe the kind of passion that seared Wordsworth's soul in the Annette period. There are some stirrings of the animal spirits of the great Dorothy period we have not yet analyzed: consider the oxymoronic juxtapositions (steadiness and excess) present in Margaret's love in the first book, in which she is presented as "a Woman of a steady mind, / Tender and deep in her excess of love" (I, 513–14, *PW.*, V, 26). But the spirit of the later books is recognizable as that of the married Wordsworth meditating on life, love, and loss, on aspects of his own personality and being, from the usually unruffled state of domesticity. Into that uxorial peace the body thrusts itself again and again. Sometimes Wordsworth keeps the body present from earlier inspirations. Margaret, for example, that finely realized figure of pathos, makes poignantly clear the importance to happiness of the flesh as it suffers progressive loss: with loss of husband comes loss of bodily pleasure and Wordsworth makes it a piercing pity. "Her body was subdued. . . . / . . . no motion of the breast was seen, / No heaving of the heart" (I, 795, 800–801; *PW.*, V, 35). When the Solitary appears, the man with "an intense and glowing mind" (II, 274; *PW.*, V, 52), surely in part a Wordsworthian avatar, whose gloomy skepticism, however, is badly in need of correction, the text introduces materials about married life closely parallel to the poet's own. Wordsworthian love, like so much human love, brings anxiety, and the lover imagines the death of the beloved; and indeed the wife does die soon, a woman of "bright form" (III, 481, *PW.*, V, 89), "silver voice" (482), and "mild radiance" (503). These phrases might easily have been directly applied to Mary, as indeed could the following procession of adjectives, not perhaps calculated to stir a modern heart but at the very heart of the poet's sensibility: she was "Young, modest, meek, and beautiful" (III, 514, *PW.*, V, 91). With her husband this "blooming Lady—a Conspicuous flower" (187) enjoyed walks in nature and was animated by "full . . . joy" and "free . . . love" (196) (uncensored feelings, bubbling up naturally?); and when the children (a girl and a boy) came, she presided over a nuclear family, isolated and blissful in a new Eden sufficient unto itself. But when the children died, "heirs of our united love; / Graced mutually by difference of sex" (590–91), first the girl and then the boy, as in Wordsworth's own grievous loss, the mother became "Calm as a frozen lake" (650) and melted in his arms shortly thereafter when death released her spirit. Before tragedy had struck it had been a beautiful conjugal scene, the kind so rarely portrayed in Western literature, on which the sun was wont to shine.

What happened when the echoing green was darkened? It is clear, whatever denials the Solitary now imposes upon himself, that Wordsworth ultimately retained his belief in "fostering Nature" (809) and in the importance of the body and its energies.

> Oh! what a joy it were, in vigorous health,
> To have a body (this our vital frame) . . .
> what a joy to roam
> An equal among mightiest energies.
>
> [IV, 508–509, 531–32, *PW.*, V, 125]

A personal Providence is clearer now than in the earlier Wordsworth, but purely natural joys continue, loving, fruitful, fructifying, under "the great sun, earth's universal lord." There is

> participation of delight
> And a strict love of fellowship, combined.
> What other spirit can it be that prompts
> The gilded summer flies to mix and weave
> Their sports together in the solar beam,
> Or in the gloom of twilight hum their joy?—
>
> [IV, 443–48, *PW.*, V, 122]

a celebration of sexuality in creation comparable to Keats's *To Autumn* and close in intellectual content to Samuel Johnson's perceiving the basis of all benevolence in the instinctual, sexual attractions of natural life which were implanted by Providence (*Rambler*, no. 99, par. 1).

The shortest and most beautiful expression of the love that sustained Wordsworth's domestic life, which we can regard as a concentrated essence of the love letters, is appropriately the poem addressed to Mary, "She was a Phantom of Delight" (*PW.*, II, 213–14). In it the husband salutes his wife as "a perfect Woman, nobly planned," but unfortunately for a modern reader he also calls her a "machine," by which of course he means merely her body, as Hamlet did when he used the same word for his own fleshly mansion (II,ii.124). Frank McConnell has seen that the term also refers to the "whole complex process of the poet's perception" of her body.

Herbert Read's outline of the poem has the merit of clarity and completeness: Wordsworth moves in each successive stanza from sight to acquaintance to intimacy—that is, from astonishment to courtship to marriage. We can get beyond such institutional progression—and beyond too the general praise of the wife—by concentrating on the central paradoxes of the vision—for so indeed it is: Mary is a "Phantom," a "lovely Apparition," a "Spirit," mediating "something of angelic light." But she also treads a household floor, bestows "love, kisses, . . . and smiles." She demonstrates powers of leadership and possession of "a reason firm" and of a "temperate will." (Protesilaus of *Laodamia* would have nothing to complain of in this wife!) And she also has the power "To haunt, to startle, and way-lay," that last word *way-lay,* put like the others into a verbal infinitive, without boundaries, with no temporal limitations, is peculiarly delicious. It is not merely the delicate suggestions of sexual playfulness and of the protected pleasures of domestic seduction that endear the word but also the hint of solidity and permanence provided by the context. Domestic happiness is not usually rewarded with such complex poetic patterning.

Love of the intensest kind animated the Mary period, a love that was, however, controlled by stoical reason, by dedication to what Irving Babbitt called the classical *frein vital*. Controls are not usually applied to natural timidity, to bloodless placidity, and Wordsworth prayed for the reproving rod precisely because he was a Wordsworth Agonistes, a man driven to potential excess in grief and love. But the stern daughter of the Voice of God is no enemy per se of "the genial sense of youth," of love, joy, and sexuality. She wears a benignant smile, and "Flowers laugh before [her] on their beds" ("Ode to Duty," *PW.,* IV, 83–86). The delicate balance achieved in this poem between discipline and delight is the key that unlocks the amorousness of this period of domestic felicity. The married state, milder, less intense, though sexually fulfilling, was an uninterrupted extension of the pleasures of life with Dorothy, which we consider next.

Dorothy: the "One Dear State of Bliss" and Wordsworth's "High Calling"

> *Witness thou*
> *The dear companion of my lonely walk,*
> *My hope, my joy, my sister, and my friend,*
> *Or something dearer still, if reason knows*
> *A dearer thought, or in the heart of love*
> *There be a dearer name.*
>
> Wordsworth, in *Dorothy's Journals, PW.*, V, 347

> *There is creation in the eye,*
> *Nor less in all the other senses; powers*
> *They are that colour, model, and combine*
> *The things perceived with such an absolute*
> *Essential energy that we may say*
> *That those most godlike faculties of ours*
> *At one and the same moment are the mind*
> *And the mind's ministers.*
>
> Wordsworth, Notebook fragment, *PW.*, V, 343

From the "substantial world" of antecedent literature in which can grow tendrils "strong as flesh and blood," Wordsworth chose the following for especial emphasis:

> Two shall be named, pre-eminently dear,—
> The gentle Lady married to the Moor;
> And heavenly Una with her milk-white Lamb.
>
> ["Personal Talk," lines 40–42, *PW.*, IV, 74]

If we were to assimilate these to the women in Wordsworth's own life, Spenser's Una, from the first book of the *Faerie Queene,* would have to be associated with his wife Mary, an association, indeed, made, though indirectly, by the poet himself. In Shakespeare's Desdemona, if the speculation is not too bold, may be seen the lineaments of the deserted Annette, against whom, in a few profound ways that did not involve jealousy, Wordsworth played a passionate and ultimately cruel Othello-role. To select a literary parallel for Dorothy we must go outside the three lines just quoted, to Milton, over whose portrayal of the expulsion from the garden in the eleventh book of *Paradise Lost* the brother and sister "melted into tears" (*Journals,* 106). For it was Milton who gave unrivaled embodiment to the Edenic bower, which the home and life in Grasmere frequently recalled. But perhaps after all the best locus for Dorothy is not a book but nature, for the poetry dedicated to her and inspired by her partakes of the impulses that seemed to "roll" through her, to use a favorite Wordsworthian verb for the movement of natural energy. Wordsworth's personification of nature as woman does not invoke the age-old topos of the alma mater nor is it, I believe, instinct with memories of his own mother lost in childhood. It is, rather, Dorothy—child, girl, and woman, muse and friend—who is the chief begetter and sustainer of the great Wordsworthian persona, Nature. It is she who blends with daffodils and sounding cataracts and with "natural" people too, like the Highland lass whom the poet addresses:

> I would have
> Some claim upon thee, if I could, . . .
> Thy elder Brother I would be,
> Thy Father—anything to thee!
> ["To a Highland Girl," lines 56–57, 60–61, PW., III, 74]

Over the Wordsworthian landscape move, not stately matrons or the nymphs of Titian and Claude, whom Keats loved, but fresh young country girls, nubile, blooming, flower-like.

Of the problems that this insinuation of Dorothy into nature and of nature into her raises about the brother-sister relationship I shall have something to say presently. Now it is important to emphasize that the sexual energies that the poet seems to find in nature must of course have been imposed by him, by that virile, strongly sensual person we confronted at the outset. And these energies must have first entered his emotional transactions with nature without any embarrassing or otherwise impeding awareness, for they were largely compounded of glad animal movements and unconscious desires. Later, as we have seen, the underlying sexuality could enter the critical sentences of discursive prose, and some of the poetry deliberately cultivates an imagistic significance that is quite explicitly sexual. But the synthesis, the coalescing of imagination and appetite (when "deep feelings had impressed / Great objects on his mind" and when he was being prepared to receive "the lesson deep of love" [*The Ruined Cottage,* lines 81–82, 116; PW., V, 381, 382]), must have begun on a level well below that of conscious construction.

The great synthesis of psychological subject and natural object that underlies the earlier versions of the *Prelude*—present in passages that are often allowed to remain in even the 1850 edition—is frequently expressed in language whose sexual resonance has seldom been acknowledged. It would be unnatural of nature to be ascetic; it would be perverse if "the bond of union betwixt love and joy" (1799 *Prelude*, I, 390; *Prel.*, 11) were free of physical cathexis. The imagery always seems to point overtly away from the obvious coupling of desiring bodies. But how often such unions and the bodily passions are indirectly suggested by trope, descriptive word, rhythm, and incident! The boy with panting heart and beating bosom is overpowered by "strong desire / Resistless" as he reaches up to steal a captive bird belonging to another, whereupon "Low breathings" among the solitary hills pursue him (lines 42–43, 47). The stealing of a boat is presented an "an act of stealth / And troubled pleasure"—suggestions enforced by the boat "heaving through the water like a swan," a bird image that we have seen and shall again see associated with the sexual (line 90–91, 106). The "intercourse of touch" (1799 *Prelude*, II, 312) extends far beyond the child at the breast; in his seventeenth year the boy reacts to nature "with bliss ineffable," as earlier he had lain on the "genial pillow of the earth, . . . soothed by a sense of touch" (1805 *Prelude*, II, 419, I, 88–89; *Prel.*, 86, 32). He strayed "voluptuously through fields and rural walks" for "it was a time of rapture" and of "giddy bliss" that "like a tempest works along the blood" (I, 253, 457, 611–12). Such language has all the marks of the libidinal about it and could scarcely be conceived as produced by a eunuch. It is extended to the coming of poetry, as the author

> kindled with the stir,
> The fermentation and the vernal heat
> Of poesy, affecting private shades
> Like a sick lover.
>
> [IV, 93–96]

Erotic feeling beats insistently even if it cannot be said to boil or seethe beneath the blank verse of the *Prelude*. Examples could be multiplied: it will suffice here to notice that the crucial moment during the first vacation from Cambridge when the poet feels himself "a dedicated spirit" follows a night of dancing and prattle:

> Slight shocks of young love-liking interspersed
> That mounted up like joy into the head,
> And tingled through the veins.
>
> [IV, 325–27]

Wordsworthian joy should never be totally separated from such tinglings. The sexual basis of poetic art, however dreamlike, is deeply if obscurely sensed. The "beauteous pictures" arising in "harmonious imagery"

94

>   left
> Obscurely mingled with their passing forms
> A consciousness of animal delight,
> A self-possession felt in every pause
> And every gentle movement of my frame.
>
>   [IV, 395–99]

Such vital and kinaesthetic energy, "dumb yearnings, hidden appetites" (V, 530), never deserted the best poetry of this master. From the placid orthodoxies of the later laureate, to be sure, they seem to be absent, though a turn of phrase or thought can now and then recall them as from a great distance.

If such staminal powers as these animate the vision of nature, some kind of clashing crisis is inevitable. *Rapture* and *rapt,* words used obsessively by Wordsworth about natural joys, are related to *rape*; and *Nutting (PW.,* II, 211–12), probably composed in late 1798, is a powerful, even a shocking and disturbing poem, to which such words are applicable. Accoutred quaintly in cast-off clothes, the poet as a boy comes to an untouched bower, a kind of Eden, "one dear nook / Unvisited." As poet recounting the experience, he insists at once on a sexual metaphor (the trees stand "Tall and erect, with tempting clusters hung, / A virgin scene!"), and he presents himself as "Voluptuous, fearless of a rival" as he "eyed / The banquet." For a brief moment he has refuge in romance—he plays with the flowers and hears the murmur of "fairy water-breaks"—a strategy typical of both the erotic Keats and the erotic Wordsworth in vacant and voluptuous moods. But then comes a spasm of sexual violence:

>   up I rose,
> And dragged to earth both branch and bough, with crash
> And merciless ravage,

leaving the nook "mutilated," "Deformed and sullied," the last word reminding us, though perhaps not Wordsworth, of the "too, too sullied flesh" of Hamlet.

Literary context of sorts is provided by the attack on the trees of the forest by the love-crazed Orlando of Ariosto's epic, but the differences outweigh the similarities. The true context for *Nutting* is provided by Wordsworth himself, by the nature he knew, and by Dorothy, who is deeply involved in this recollection. After reporting the violation of nature's virginity he has inflicted, he turns to her and bids her "move along these shades / In gentleness of heart; with gentle hand / Touch —for there is a spirit in the woods." These lines do more than enforce a cautionary moral that urges us to be gentle, and Wordsworth is far from turning away from all sexual contact, which it is one purpose of his verse to show can be decent and tender. "Touch," he tells his sister; "with gentle hand," of course; but "touch," Dorothy, "touch!"

Dorothy is even more deeply involved in another version of the scene, one not sent on to Coleridge and not a part of the publication of *Nutting* in 1800 (*PW.*, II, 504–506). In this version the girl is imagined, at least fleetingly, as the ravisher; and the exhorter to calm and gentleness is the poet himself, speaking without the sexual metaphors prominent in the final version. But he is disturbed by this vision of his sister

> with that keen look
> Half cruel in its eagerness, those cheeks
> Thus flushed with a tempestuous bloom,
> I might have almost deem'd that I had pass'd
> A houseless being in a human shape,
> An enemy of nature.
>
> [lines 8–13]

The two versions show that even in this recollection of sexually troped violence toward nature William is mingling or even exchanging identities with Dorothy; and it is fair to say that it was not always true, as he said of her in the *Prelude,* that

> thy breath,
> Dear sister, was a kind of gentler spring
> That went before my steps.
>
> [1805 *Prelude,* XIII, 244–46]

The night before his wedding (a ceremony that Dorothy was emotionally incapable of attending, though she was nearby) Wordsworth gave her the wedding ring to keep until the morning. She wore it on her forefinger, and the next day she gave it back to him with what she called "how deep a blessing." He then "slipped it again onto my finger and blessed me fervently." Wordsworth's best biographer, who quotes these words, calls this private ceremony "a sacramental renewal of an unbreakable fidelity." It was followed by a lifetime in the home of the Wordsworths passed, in unclouded friendship and love, with Mary and her children. It was preceded by a period of unmatched creativity, when the poet produced some of the tenderest love poetry in our language, all addressed to Dorothy or inspired by her.

All of the above and more—in addition to the fact that there seemed to have been something in current and immediately antecedent culture that was tolerant toward brother-sister incest (Shelley called it "like many other *incorrect* things a very poetical circumstance")—has laid suspicion on the relations of the poet to his sister. The late Lord Kenneth Clark, in a popular television series on Romantic art, seemed to take abnormality between the Wordsworths for granted and drew what I regard as a tasteless and unwarranted parallel between them and Lord Byron and his sister Augusta. The imputation of overt incest has been called ludicrous, lurid, inappropriate, mischievous; to this list of angry words I would add *difficult,* if not *impossible,* to conceive. Dorothy's journals show that the deep love Wordsworth revealed in his life, letters, and poetry was fully reciprocated. Their life together before Wordsworth's marriage was one of devotion, tenderness, and intimacy, with scenes of some physical contact like caressing and kissing and of tender proximities at not inappropriate moments. And when there was excess of feeling—as there certainly was when Dorothy could not find it in herself to throw into the fire the remainder of an apple into which her brother had bitten (*Journals,* 119)—the excess is sentimental and mawkish, not sensual and morbid. Moreover, the house was a bustle of activity: neighbors and friends from far and near came in and out, sometimes staying for long periods. Dove Cottage was a place of incessant, strenuous, symptom-producing work for the poet, who just before his marriage went through one of his most fertile and exacting poetic periods. The taboo was still too strong in the Romantic period in England to have been challenged by such friendly, hospitable, rural, relaxed, and, on one level, conventional people. When they did not reveal the qualities I have just listed, the Wordsworths were either overworked or suffering from very common ailments like aches in the head or stomach.

And yet the love was fervent indeed. If the thesis of this chapter has validity—that physicality was an essential ingredient of Wordsworthian nature and entered almost every emotion that touched the poet's psyche —then we must expect that sexual attraction of some kind found a place here too, mostly natural and unaware but capable of coming to the surface of the poet's mind.

I may have overstressed the conventionality of the circle in order to obviate what inevitably gets in the way of a discussion of Wordsworthian love, the charge or hint of overt incest. But I have to concede that guilt and potential danger did lurk in the relationship: we have already seen Dorothy imaginatively implicated in the aggressively sexual poem *Nutting.* In *Tintern Abbey* the sister, with her "wild eyes," is associated with the period of "dizzy raptures" and "wild ecstasies" in the love of nature (lines 85, 119, 138, *PW.,* II, 261–63). Although many poems to Emma or Emmeline, poetic names for Dorothy, the dear person he also called his "sweet friend" (1805 *Prelude,* XIII, 227), are simple, sensuous, and sincere in their expressions of tender love, many are darkly disturbed with the thought of death. Such are the justly admired Lucy poems, products of the early Dorothy period in Wordsworth's creative life.

In the alternative version of *Nutting* the poet addresses his sister as Lucy (line 6, *PW.*, II, 505), and I have come to agree with those who see Dorothy behind the shadowy figure who, in the short but multi-layered, severe but mysterious lyrics, haunts the borders between rural reality and a dream. In these poems Lucy is imagined as dying, but I cannot agree with the late F.W. Bateson that Wordsworth now solved the threatening relationship with his sister "by killing her off symboli-cally." To *kill off* strikes me as unnecessarily sensational and blunt, and Donald Reiman's subtler approach is surely closer to the truth. He be-lieves that Lucy is allowed to die so that she cannot be united in a for-bidden relationship and that the author shifts his imaginative stance from brother to lover to avoid focusing his sexual drive on a sister. Such a view has the merit of showing the psychic complexity that underlies the verse and of providing a basis for the rich mythography inscribed in these short lyrics.

Though sexuality comes in soon enough, it should not provide the first perspective. As we have seen, Wordsworth sometimes imagined, though often very indirectly, the death of those he loved the most intensely—perhaps Mary, even himself, and Mary and himself together:

> O sacred marriage-bed of death,
> That keeps them side by side
> In bond of peace, in bond of love,
> That may not be untied!
> ["George and Sarah Green," 1808, *PW.*, IV, 376]

Dorothy—we must say particularly Dorothy—was not exempted from these intimations of mortality. That profound little poem, "'Tis said, that some have died for love," portrays a strong man brought so low by suffering over the death of his "pretty Barbara" that beholding the eglantine once loved together "Disturbs me till the sight is more than I can bear." Wordsworth makes a quiet identification of himself with the sufferer, fearing a like fate for himself; and then turning to his sister he exclaims in pain,

> Ah gentle love! if ever thought was thine
> To store up kindred hours for me, thy face
> Turn from me, gentle Love! nor let me walk
> Within the sound of Emma's voice, nor know
> Such happiness as I have known to-day.
> [lines 48–52, *PW.*, II, 34]

But if indeed Emma-Dorothy should die, what consolations then? The answer lies in the Lucy poems, which begin in "strange fits of passion" and end in the girl's death into nature, with the following paradoxically different results imagined. (1) She may become a part of "earth's diurnal round"—

> No motion has she now, no force;
> She neither hears nor sees—
>
> ["A slumber did my spirit seal," *PW.*, II, 216]

in which case she has achieved a state directly antithetical to the poet's earthly passion, which may have been so feverish as to require an insensate termination. (2) Or she may, more complexly and paradoxically, have become at once calm and wild, capable of being "sportive as the fawn" but also wrapped in "the silence . . . of mute insensate things." Climactically, the dead but imaginatively resurrected girl becomes a mature sexual being,

> 'And vital feelings of delight
> Shall rear her form to stately height,
> Her virgin bosom swell.'
>
> ["Three years she grew," line 31–33, *PW.*, II, 215]

Nature speaks here; and when she says, "Such, *thoughts* to Lucy I will give" (line 34, emphasis added), she invokes the poetic process. Lucy's death is thus swallowed up in victory through the myth of a sexually vital nature. Dorothy has not been "killed off." In one sense she has not even died. Her stately height and virgin bosom have now become available as a muse is available to the creating mind—more precisely, as an imaginatively created myth can turn back to its creator and renew his energy. Such energy is released when the *données* of reality become imaginative data living on in the mind. That is the high fate of the sexual Dorothy.

The Lucy poems were composed away from England, in Goslar, Germany, in late 1798 or early 1799. Lucy-Dorothy is thought of not as a little child but as a girl three-years grown into a love-relationship who then dies. In the first surviving portion of Wordsworth's great unfinished poem, *The Recluse,* dating from the first spring in Grasmere, 1800, the beloved is a woman, for all intents and purposes a wife, the occupant of a shared nest, a place described in the 1805 *Prelude* as providing "one dear state of bliss," the "dear delight" that surpasses all other human joy and that stands at the very top of Wordsworth's hierarchy of conscious pleasure—his chief intensity, as it were:

99

The bliss of walking daily in life's prime
Through field or forest with the maid we love
While yet our hearts are young, while yet we breathe
Nothing but happiness, living in some place,
Deep vale, or anywhere the home of both
From which it would be misery to stir.

[XII, 127, 129–34, 136; *Prel.* 444]

These lines from the *Prelude* could, I suppose, be taken to refer to life
with Mary, but their youthful glow, the sense of isolation, the untroubled
happiness, and the presence of only two seem to point primarily to the
period we are now concerned with. They join the lines from the *Home
at Grasmere* (the part written in 1800) now to be analyzed to celebrate
life in the vale of Grasmere with Dorothy. Did we not know from history both the dwelling-place and the blood-kinship of the inhabitants,
the poetry itself would lead us to exclaim: here the nuclear family has
found its poetic celebrant at last!

Wordsworth certainly speaks of the beloved spot as a proprietor
would:

The unappropriated bliss hath found
An owner, and that owner I am he.
The Lord of this enjoyment is on Earth
And in my breast. What wonder if I speak
With fervour, am exalted with the thought
Of my possessions?

[*Home at Grasmere*, MS. B, lines 85–90; p. 42]

Wordsworth is himself the small owner of a rural plot, the kind of life
he saw as the best preserver of the domestic affections. But he is also
Adam—more precisely a new Adam, a second Adam, to use Pauline
language. Originally, among "the bowers / Of blissful Eden," there was
not, he says, the "possession of the good," the realized imagination, or
the fulfilled "ancient thought" that he now owns in "highest measure"
(*Home,* lines 122–28, p. 44). Why is Wordsworth's the higher boon, "absolute," of "surpassing grace" (ibid.), higher even than the prelapsarian?
Not, I believe, for Christian reasons, for Christ never enters this picture. *Grace* is, however, not unimportant, for the poet is not a primal
innocent; he has known loss and grief, suffering and sin, from which
he has been mercifully rescued. But still the Edenic parallel remains
cogent. Even though we are later made aware that the couple are not
alone and that "Society is here: / The true community," he nevertheless
regards himself as "peacefully embowered" (*Home,* lines 76, p. 43; and
818–19, p. 90). And his partner, whom he describes with historical accuracy as

100

> A younger orphan of a Home extinct,
> The only Daughter of my Parents,
>
> [*Home*, MS. D, lines 78–79, p. 43]

must be regarded as his beloved Eve. The very language that follows recalls *Paradise Lost*: the poet says he never lingered over "a lovely object"

> But either She whom now I have, who now
> Divides with me this loved abode, was there
> Or not far off. Where'er my footsteps turned,
> Her Voice was like a hidden Bird that sang;
> The thought of her was like a flash of light
> Or an unseen companionship, a breath
> Of fragrance independent of the wind.
>
> [*Home*, MS. B, lines 107–13, p. 44]

I have mentioned *Paradise Lost,* but this Eve does not wish to wander
off for a bit of separate but equal gardening nor does this Eden seem
in any way threatened by a Fall.

The question forces itself upon us — can we avoid bringing to mind
the lovely sexual dalliance of the Miltonic Eden? Since Wordsworth has
confessed without embarrassment or strain to proper, though intense,
sororal relations with his Eve, here called by Dorothy's poetic name "my
Emma," any sexual allusion would have to be exquisitely indirect. But
present it seems indeed to be. In poetry of a very high order Wordsworth
evokes bird-imagery and bird-calls in describing the pair, and we remember that such imagery was beautifully applied to Vaudracour and Julia,
made by the poet the poetic equivalents of Wordsworth and Annette
Vallon. Here the poetry is even tenderer — and better:

> Long is it since we met to part no more,
> Since I and Emma heard each other's call
> And were Companions once again, like Birds
> Which by the intruding Fowler had been scared,
> Two of a scattered brood that could not bear
> To live in loneliness.
>
> [*Home*, lines 171–76, p. 48]

Wordsworth also compares himself and Dorothy to two "milk-white
Swans" who failed one Spring to appear at their usual retreat in the center
of the lake, even though they had come daily during two months of
"unrelenting storm." The birds are especially dear because "their state
so much resembled ours":

> They also having chosen this abode,
> They strangers, and we strangers; they a pair,

And we a solitary pair like them.
They should not have departed.
[*Home,* MS. B, lines 323, 330, 338, 339–42, p. 58]

The tenderness of that last sentence is piercing—in his heart of hearts the poet does not want the orphan brother and sister ever to leave their retreat.

Could swan-imagery for Wordsworth be entirely free of uxorial if not sexual content? Keats used swans in his poetry with overt sexual meaning—a poetic habit sanctioned by Jove who turned himself into one to woo Leda, and by Spenser, who introduced them into his *Prothalamion,* where their satin whiteness and bright beauty shone "Against [a] Brydale day, which was not long." Wordsworth in the *Salisbury Plain* poem quoted earlier had made his swans erotic, with heaving bosoms "soft and white." Guilt and sorrow over Annette may have entered those earlier lines; but there is no trace of morbidity here or even of present or past grief. There is, however, a touch of self-consciousness in applying the swan imagery to the siblings at Dove Cottage. In an early draft these birds seem to have been male and female, husband and wife, for they are called "partners"; and when one is imagined to have been killed, the other lives "in its widowhood." In a heavy cancellation that leaves these lines still readable, Wordsworth removes the distinction of sex, and the two become "Companions, brethren, consecrated friends." In the final version these companions "Inseparable" in "constant love" are no longer even "brethren" but only "consecrated friends, Faithful Companions." Such changes could not help being deliberate, and we thus know that at least once the conscious mind of Wordsworth revised away sexually suggestive language that he had applied to his relations with Dorothy, though he did so with the full knowledge of his copyists, Mary and Dorothy.

John Beer sees Grasmere with Dorothy alone as a prelude to Grasmere with Dorothy and Mary, the intense love continuing from the smaller to the slightly larger community, "where the quiet work of the mature human heart, anchored in a deeply physical love, could contain, and find a place for, more intense and extreme attachments." The comment on the physical anchor of sentimental love is admirably just, but could there be anything more spiritually intense or extreme than the poet's attachment to his sister, and was there ever again so rich an outpouring of immortal verse as during the Dorothy years?

It is appropriate to conclude with an apocalypse. The vision on Mount Snowdon has been much studied but has never, I believe, been regarded as a climactic expression of the poet's encounter with earthly love. The episode begins physically enough, with language that evokes a strongly kinetic sense: "Thus did we breast the ascent":

> With forehead bent,
> Earthward, as if in opposition set
> Against an enemy, I panted up
> With eager pace.
>
> [1805 *Prelude,* XIII, 20, 29–32; *Prel.,* 458]

Here the earth is felt to be a foe, but the language establishes it as a real presence before its transcendence is contemplated. The vision may be said to begin when a light "Fell like a flash" upon the turf. At once re-establishing his own presence, the poet writes,

> I looked about, and lo,
> The moon stood naked in the heavens, at height
> Immense above my head,
>
> [XIII, 40–42]

and we have entered the first phase of the experience. The moon is not alone the subject of contemplation, for at the poet's feet the mist rests like a sea, while hundreds of hills, like waves in that sea, upheave "their dusky backs" (line 45). So both mist and hill are not just vaguely organic but are giant bodies, appropriately accompanying the immensity overhead. There is no doubt who dominates: "the moon looked down upon this shew / In single glory" (lines 52–53).

The moon of the Romantics' delight has emerged in much great poetry and painting, and Wordsworth himself had often personified the lesser light as a woman, loved in childhood, associated with passion and the death of a beloved girl in the Lucy poems, and contemplated languidly as she hung between the hills of home "as if she knew / No other region but belonged to thee, / Yea, appertained by a peculiar right / To thee and thy grey huts, my darling vale" (1805 *Prelude,* II, 199–202; *Prel.,* 74, 76). And we recall Keats's "Queen-Moon . . . on her throne / Cluster'd around by all her starry Fays" in the *Nightingale* ode (lines 36–37). Blake, in a beautiful water-color illustration to *Il Penseroso,* portrays a lovely moon-maiden above the melancholy poet's head — she long-haired, delicate-featured, full-breasted, bare-footed but not nude, for she wears a gauzy gown and trencher. But neither Keats, nor Blake, nor the Wordsworth of the other passages cited rivals in power the arresting, solitary, nude female figure who dominates the night sky on Snowdon. How can she fail to be an overpowering sexual presence? "I looked about, and lo, / The Moon stood naked in the heavens at height / Immense above my head" (XIII, 40–41).*

---

*The 1850 revision of these lines reads: "The Moon hung naked in a firmament / Of azure without cloud," lines which lose the effectiveness of the earlier version. The conventional and classical "hung," which undoubtedly attracted Wordsworth as an in-

The other even more astounding image in this vision is the breach
in the mist, in which the poet places the presence of God. If I have been
right so far about the physical, even the kinaesthetic, realities of the scene,
we must regard this great opening as also being palpably sensed: a third
of a mile away (observe how typically exact Wordsworth's measurements
are even here!)

> Was a blue chasm, a fracture in the vapour,
> A deep and gloomy breathing-place, through which
> Mounted the roar of waters, torrents, streams,
> Innumerable, roaring, with one voice. . . .
> in that breach
> Through which the homeless voice of waters rose,
> That dark deep thoroughfare, had Nature lodged
> The soul, the imagination of the whole.
>
> [lines 56–59, 62–65]

The senses primarily appealed to are the eye and the ear, though it should
be pointed out that the roar of many waters could easily penetrate to
the poet's ear through the vapors and that he must have wanted a clearly
visible breach for its power of suggestiveness. What does it suggest? All
the words used to describe it are strong—and unusual in Wordsworth:
chasm, fracture, breathing-place, thoroughfare. There is an Alpine scene
in one of Wordsworth's very earliest poems, *Descriptive Sketches,* that
anticipates the Snowdon sea of mists and its corridor of sound—"a single
chasm, a gulf of gloomy blue" that gaped in the center of that earlier
vapory sea, through which a roaring sound of innumerable streams arose.
The image of a skyey chasm had thus been in Wordsworth's mind from an
early date, and De Quincey has somewhere testified that it was a characteristic feature of cloud and mist in the Lake District sky. Wordsworth
much later, writing rather blandly about sin, said that "Pain entered
through a ghastly breach." We human beings enter life through a canal
and then a breach; and it is difficult not to feel—so powerful is Wordsworth's juxtaposition of images here—that the fracture and the breach*

---

trinsically poetic verb, seems here to weaken the force of "stood" by making it impossible to visualize a hanging woman, and the placid "azure" removes the physicality of
"height / Immense above my head" (1850 *Prelude,* XIV, 40–41, *Prel.,* 461). Was the older
Wordsworth too tame to tolerate a powerful sexual presence?

The word *naked* occurs frequently enough in Wordsworth to describe, mostly, rocks,
stones, cliffs but also heaths, pools, walls, trees, the heavens. History, truth, the instincts
can be naked, as is the soul (personified as female) in the presence of her God. Indians
are more than once called naked. In the only clear instance of the application of the adjective to a single human being, it means unarmed. It therefore compels attention when
Wordsworth calls a female personification standing large and alone "naked."

*changed to *rift,* a more timid word, by the older Wordsworth in the 1850 *Prelude*
(XIV, 56, *Prel.,* 461).

in the mists, seen as being below the nude woman of the night sky, are somehow related to her large and inescapable body. Since grotesque visualizing could easily take over, I wish to be as indirect and purely suggestive as Wordsworth is, without missing his meaning or losing the immense power of the description.

Even if we only half believe in the poet's literalness here, we must surely feel that he is suggesting that sexuality, birth, the body itself, and its orifices, somehow support, accommodate, or even produce ultimately "the soul, the imagination of the whole" (line 65). Soon after describing this vision Wordsworth speaks directly, without imagery, about the location in man of primal vitality:

> The prime and vital principle is thine
> In the recesses of thy nature, far
> From any reach of outward fellowship,
> Else 'tis not thine at all.
>
> [XIII, 194–97, *Prel.*, 470]

It would be a mistake to make the *recesses* of this passage refer only to quietistic, spiritual inwardness. It suggests rather the internalization of basic sexual instinct, and something like that seems to be what the poet requires of us in contemplating the chasm on Snowdon.

When meditation on this marvelous scene arose in Wordsworth's own mind later that night, considerable eloquence remains, as in the passage just quoted; but much poetic power is lost in abstraction and mere assertion. The "dim or vast" (lines 72–73) tends to take over, and the poet seems to revert to the view, expressed occasionally elsewhere, that the light of sense must go out before we can become spirits dedicated to the One Life, to intellectual love—that the higher love is no longer "human merely" (line 164) but takes on a supramundane reality, in which the body dies so that soul can clap her hands and sing. But the central propulsive force in Wordsworth's thought during his greatest years is that man is a "creature / Sensuous and intellectual," "A Two-fold frame of body and of mind," that "This love more intellectual cannot be / Without imagination" (lines 166–67)—in other words, that imagination cannot stand without sense and that sense is meaningless and powerless without the libido. A sexless nature is a contradiction in terms, and we remember that Wordsworth even as a conservative political thinker said that "the higher mode of being necessarily includes the lower"—right down through the sentient to the animal in us. That kind of reality I have found in Wordsworth's intensest apocalypse, nobly refined but insistently present. I do not always find it in Wordsworth's grandiose rhetorical or philosophical utterances, where abstraction sometimes dulls the lineaments of desire. But on Snowdon, Wordsworth is at his most vibrant, and universal meaning is imagistically conceived as a mighty extension of energetic physical being.

Geoffrey Hartman's exciting insight into the importance to Wordsworth of the "spot-syndrome," the *omphalos,* the navel, the narrowed opening, I embrace with admiration. But I do not, like Professor Hartman, see in it an "astonishing avoidance of apocalypse," nor do I locate Wordsworth's failures in his constant return to natural fact in which he ignores the inevitable need in apocalypse of rebirth and purgation. It is true that Wordsworth rarely introduced the Christian paradox of ravishment leading to wholeness, of the death of a corn of wheat that must precede the Spring quickening. He may not have been the kind of thinker who even understood such paradoxes, to say nothing of glorying in them, as did Donne or Lancelot Andrewes. It was his greatness to mythologize the fructifying energies of nature, including the sexual, and to make them tender and human in a society that relates us to one another. Inheritor of a powerful empirical strain and also of the eighteenth-century fusion of sex and sensibility, he dismayed Coleridge—and himself too —by not being able to realize the staggering Kantian demands his friend made upon him—to write a poem that would demonstrate that the senses were essentially growths of the mind and spirit and not the other way around. Indeed, Wordsworth may have clung to the more congenial Lockean notion that the mind was formed by the senses and by reflection upon the senses, however much he modified it.

Coleridge was equally dismayed by his friend's conception of love:

> Wordsworth is by nature incapable of being in Love, tho' no man is more tenderly attached—hence he ridicules the existence of other passion, than a compound of Lust with esteem & Friendship, confined to one Object.
> [*Coll. Letters,* III, 305]

Substitute sexuality for *lust* (a tendentious word) and you have the great eighteenth-century ideal of esteem enlivened by desire. But what has Wordsworth missed? What does Coleridge want him to see? "Universal affinity" (what Freud criticized in *Civilization and its Discontents* as the "oceanic" feeling); "a long & finely graduated Scale of elective Attractions" (*Coll. Letters,* III, 305)—a concept not unlike the great Chain of Being but clearly beginning in the family; ultimately, transcendental religious love that dissolves ego-love and in human relationships effects a union of opposites that permits a *tertium quid* to appear, in which the sublimity assumes beauty, masculinity assumes femininity, and vice versa. When such deep fusion occurs, when completely new qualities emerge, then indeed the highest poetry, the product of the secondary imagination, becomes a true analogy of man and woman in love. A musically profound example of such Romantic fusion occurs in the duets of the second act of Wagner's *Tristan und Isolde,* where the lovers achieve an eternal unity of consciousness,

> Ohne Nennen, . . .
> endlos ewig
> ein – bewuszt.

Just before this *höchste Liebeslust* each lover assumes the other's identity. Tristan sings to Isolde,

> Tristan du
> ich Isolde
> nicht mehr Tristan!

And Isolde sings to Tristan,

> Du Isolde
> Tristan ich
> nicht mehr Isolde.

Such abandonment of individual identity was outside the ken of Wordsworth's vision; had it not been, he may have found the very thought repellent. Nevertheless, some notion of appropriating the beloved's essential qualities is present in Wordsworth's thought. He was aware that Dorothy had "soften[ed] down" his own "over-sternness" (1805 *Prelude,* XIII, 226–27; *Prel.,* 470) and given him a portion of her nature. But there was that within Wordsworth's genius that would not allow the boundaries of his own or others' being to be obliterated, and what he wanted in love was complementarity, not fusion into oneness.

Keeping the sexes separate and distinct, however complementary, does, as we know all too well today, risk aggression and violence, and not many of our own twentieth-century theorists of love leave much room for tenderness between sexes regarded as opposite. Wordsworth did indeed confront violence and contrast in nature and in love, as our analysis of *Nutting* has shown. And however we interpret the realities of his sororal relationship—did they ever or never constitute a carnal imagination or temptation?—they should not be allowed to tame his notions of love down to the delicateness we have seen associated with pre-Romantic or Shelleyan love of similitude. But it was his greatest achievement, in loving collaboration with Dorothy, to subdue aggression to tenderness and ultimately to be inspired by the gentlest and kindliest muse of any great poet in English. The love he celebrated arose from sexual soil, but it fell back upon the earth as a gentle rain from heaven. This poet of the primary instincts came to see that love, as well as being a passionate giving, is the receiving of a blessing in passiveness, and that it can insinuate itself like a perfume into our vital air. Dorothy too perceived that love is not primarily a task, ritual, duty, or law but the vital air of our being, which we breathe in and breathe out. It is not inappropriate that the begetter and refiner of so much that is natural, joyous, and beautiful in Wordsworthian love be given the last word. She wrote to her friend of many years, who was soon to become her sister-in-law for many, many more:

> Oh Mary my dear Sister, be quiet and happy. Study the flowers, the birds, and all the common things that are about you. Do not make loving us your business, but let your love of us make up the business you have.

4. WILLIAM BLAKE
"Arrows of Desire" and "Chariots of Fire"

*Now You will I hope shew all the family of Antique Borers, that
Peace & Plenty & Domestic Happiness is the Source of Sublime
Art, & prove to the abstract Philosophers — that Enjoyment & not
Abstinence is the food of Intellect.*
Blake to George Cumberland, 6 December 1795 (E., 700)

*SEX, according to Blake, is our most immediate and all-pervading
problem. He exalted the act as few Christians have done.*
S. Foster Damon, *A Blake Dictionary, s.v.* Sex

The greatness of Blake as poet and mythologist, now almost universally
recognized, has not often enough been perceived to extend to his treatment of sexual love, one of his obsessive themes. Yet as both poet and
painter he was never profounder or more complex — and never in greater
need of a commentator — than when he was building "Loves Temple" (*The
Everlasting Gospel,* f, line 64; E., 522), than when he was inspired by
"The Naked Human form divine, . . . / On which the Soul Expands
its wing" (lines 66, 68). At such moments Blake was at once socio-political
and personal. Few have so subtly and comprehensively explored the way
in which sexual love insinuates our public institutions and is itself insinu-
ated by them, but at the same time the myth again and again blushes red
with personal passion, with personal suffering. When the prophecy pulsates, it is surely real blood that is being propelled; and we can now and
then, though by no means often enough to satisfy curiosity, get glimpses
of actual experience behind the mythic beings and events. Catherine,
Blake's wife, his own "sweet Shadow of Delight" (*Milton* 42 [49], 28; E.,
143), is unfortunately not now available to history as Fanny Brawne and
Dorothy and Mary Wordsworth are, and we must interpret Blake's words
and designs without very much illumination from personal letters or
journals. Nevertheless, the art that expresses sexual love is compellingly
real, resting unmistakably on psychic and social fact; and it is also sophisticated, for it embodies erotic meaning both as energy ("Arrows of
desire") and as form (a "Chariot of fire") (*Milton,* Preface, E., 95).
 The present interpretation is frankly revisionist with respect to most
of those — and they are not many — who have commented separately

and extensively on my topic. I concentrate here and elsewhere on the recent book of Leopold Damrosch because its wisdom, even profundity, will make it a standard interpretation for many. This book denies the centrality—at times even the possibility—of love in Blake's thought, which is regarded as simply incapable of taking into account the reality of the other. But according to Blake's own desires at least, "the most sublime act is to set another before you" (*MHH,* plate 5, *E.,* 36), an act so difficult that the author of this sentence (almost like one from the Sermon on the Mount, though it is presented as hellish wisdom) had ultimately to call upon all the resources of the religion most congenial to him to achieve it. That religion was the heart-melting and ego-subduing Christianity of John the Apostle, and the embrace of otherness he certainly did achieve in a victory that lies behind his finally glad and ungrudging acceptance of sexuality. Sexuality ultimately came to rest comfortably in the bosom of his faith:

> And O thou Lamb of God, whom I
> Slew in my dark self-righteous pride: . . .
>
> Come to my arms & never more
> Depart; but dwell for ever here:
> Create my Spirit to thy Love:
> Subdue my Spectre to thy Fear.
>> [*Jer.,* 65–66, 69–72; *E.,* 173]

We shall see that the love sanctioned by the Lamb of God is not *agape* alone but a combination of *eros* and *agape.*

The Sexuality of Innocence: "Love, . . . Peace, and Raptures Holy"

Infancy, fearless, lustful, happy! nestling for delight
In laps of pleasure; Innocence! honest, open, seeking
The vigorous joys of morning light; open to virgin
*   bliss.*
> Blake, VDA., 6:4–6; E., 49

The salute of Blake's revolutionary female mover and shaker, Oothoon, to "fearless, lustful, happy" infancy and to "honest, open" Innocence gives us the proper perspective on what preoccupied her creator from at least as early as 1777 until about 1789, when the volume of *Songs* displaying the innocent state of the human soul first appeared. Innocence, far from being merely a state to pass through, is in fact a foundation for later individual and racial behavior and enters profoundly into many of Blake's most complex and rewarding formulations. Oothoon's perspective is far from being Freudian, since the childhood being celebrated (of course both literal and imaginative) does not fester with future neurosis. Sexuality in Blakean Innocence is rather a carryover into Romantic sensibility of the relaxation the Enlightenment felt in contemplating primitive behavior. "Creep away," said Diderot's noble and despairing old native, "into the dark forest, if you wish, with the perverse companions of your pleasures, but allow the good, simple Tahitians to reproduce themselves without shame under the open sky and in broad daylight." Blake's youths and maidens in their age of gold enjoy their "kisses sweet" while they "Naked in the sunny beams delight" ("A Little Girl Lost," lines 9, 20; *E.*, 29); and the poet continued for several years (though not always, as we shall see) to commend open, daylight, unafraid, and unself-conscious relationships. The later Blake once deplored the voluptuousness that he thought came in with the Renaissance ("A Descriptive Catalogue, p. 12, *E.*, 533); but in his celebration of the natural sexuality of Innocence, he can be observed transforming Shakespearean bawdy into uninhibited but guiltless delight. Pandarus of *Troilus and Cressida* (III. i. 116–21) in the midst of uttering transparent double-entendres plays on the common sexual meaning of death, transmuting the longing for the female O to immediate and laughing fulfillment:

> These lovers cry— O ho they die!
>   Yet that which seems the wound to kill,
> Doth turn O ho, to Ha, ha, he!
>   So dying love lives still.
> O ho, a while but Ha, ha, ha!
> O ho, groans out for Ha, ha, ha!

In the lightly suggestive "Laughing Song" of *Innocence* steamy adult licentiousness has disappeared, and healthy sexuality remains as a group of fully clothed adolescents sit around a table *en plein air* and lift their wine glasses while "their sweet round mouths sing *Ha*, Ha, He" (*E.*, 11).

If we go back to consider Blake's first published work, the *Poetical Sketches* (printed in 1783), we can see that he has developed, out of some of the same literary materials that Keats used, a type of active eroticism* quite unlike the younger poet's languorous and luxuriant sensu-

---

*but not so suggestive or allusive a one as Nelson Hilton has discovered. I welcome him as an ally in seeing sexuality in these early poems, but I find that the assimilation of "valleys" to *vulva* and of the dew in "dewy locks" to genital juices, especially semen, is extreme. I would not have joined the three students who walked out of his class at these suggestions, but I take this opportunity of saying that they could easily destroy the delicacy of these lyrics. See "Some Sexual Connotations" in *Blake: An Illustrated Quarterly* 16 (Winter 1982–83): 166.

ality. Central to Blake's are natural personifications of sexually potent males—the robust, aggressive Summer, with his "ruddy limbs and flourishing hair" (*E.,* 409), a kind of proto-Orc who also anticipates Blake's Poet-Shepherd. This category also includes, to reach forward a bit, the "Youth of delight" of *The Songs of Experience* ("The Voice of the Ancient Bard," *E.,* 31), who witnesses the "opening morn," and the golden-haired and bright-formed "Cloud" of *The Book of Thel,* who is capable of dalliance with the willing fair-eyed Dew. In need of higher sanctions than Shakespeare, Spenser, or nature can provide, Blake endows the King Lion of "The Little Girl Lost" and "The Little Girl Found" (originally poems of *Innocence*) with sexual potency and tolerance and with the suggestion that he is also Christ, the lion of the tribe of Judah, a "spirit arm'd in gold" (*E.,* 22), a color which the poet-painter often associated with the erotic as well as the prophetic.

Aggressiveness is not confined to male personifications. Without deserting the delicate shyness so much loved in pre-Romantic sensibility, Blake gives a "languish'd head" as well as "modest tresses" to his Spring, who is supplicated by "longing eyes" in a "love-sick land" (*E.,* 408); and Morning, a "holy virgin," is asked to "salute the sun," personified as a huntsman aroused for the chase (*E.,* 410–11). Blake does not usually allow his maidens to languish (as does the woman in "My Silks and Fine Array" [*E.,* 413] in frustration over a cold and unresponsive male), but he tends to set them in motion on quests for experience. Of Thel, Ona, Oothoon, and Lyca, only the last two succeed in breaking away from convention, though in the case of the first two it is most likely that convention (and not the girls) is to blame. In the story "The Little Girl Lost . . . and Found" Lyca leaves her parents not without pain and fear but ends up nude and presumably "innocently" experienced in a natural paradise with lions and other beasts of prey, a clear adumbration of the Blakean Beulah (on which much more later). What Blake's verbal-visual scene (Plate XIII) recalls is Isaiah's prophetic vision—with this important addendum, that the girl Lyca, once lost but now found, and her ménage of children and animals in suggestive poses unmistakably invoke Innocent sexuality. To quote the climax line of Conrad Aiken's marvelous adaptation of Isaiah, "the loin lies down with the limb."*

---

*The limerick deserves to be quoted in full:
> It's time to make love: douse the glim,
> the fireflies twinkle and dim,
>   the stars lean together
>   like birds of a feather
> and the loin lies down with the limb.
> Quoted in *American Scholar,*
> Summer 1980, p. 413.

PLATE XIII. William Blake, "The Little Girl Found," *Songs of Innocence and of Experience,* copy N.

In moving the women of his early poetry from traditional sexual passivity to amorous search or to leadership in sex-roles and functions, Blake was heeding important voices in his own milieu. Mary Wollstonecraft was a direct influence and Richard Payne Knight a suggestive parallel. The latter was not entirely free of stereotypes (he talks about "the mild sensibility of passive courage" that naturally becomes "the weaker sex"), but at the same time he preached to women the need for health of body, "mental affection," and "vigour," setting up as examples Homer's Nausicaa and Fielding's Sophia Western. He encouraged the expression of energy, exertion of mind and body, and passionate action — as did Blake.

Revolutionary Sexuality

The harvest shall flourish in wintry weather
When two virginities meet together

The King & the Priest must be tied in a tether
Before two virgins can meet together
Blake, "Merlins Prophecy," E., 473

Children of the future Age,
Reading this indignant page;
Know that in a former time.
Love! sweet love! was thought a crime.
Blake, "A Little Girl Lost," Songs of Experience; E., 29

Revolutionary sexuality grows directly out of Innocence, where appetite is natural, childlike, unfettered — and dangerous when frustrated. Innocence itself does not apply the inhibition, society does — and the complications in Experience are enormous. We should not allow the direct and fresh force of Blakean libido directed at society to be burdened now with his later fear "Lest the Sexual Generation swallow up Regeneration" (*Jer.*, 90: 37, E., 250). Blake's culture provided examples of outwardly mobile women-leaders and also domestically dominant women. Rousseau's Julie in *La Nouvelle Heloïse* was a widely admired example of the wife as leader and educator, but she is frigidity itself when compared with Blake's passionate Oothoon; and few lovers produced by sensibility or Romanticism have the instinctual fire of Blake's Orc, "intense! naked! a Human fire fierce glowing" (*Amer.*, 4: 8; E., 53). The two most vigorous Lambeth prophecies, the *Visions of the Daughters of Albion* and *America,* which open respectively the gates of courtship to "lovely copulation bliss on bliss" (*VDA.*, 7: 26; E., 50) and the doors of marriage to "females naked and glowing with the lusts of youth"

(*Amer.*, 15: 22; *E.*, 57), both begin with consummated sexual acts. When "fiery desire" and "high-breathing joy" seize the revolutionary activist, they invade the whole body—"the feet / Hands, head, bosom, and parts of love" (*The French Revolution*, lines 183–85; *E.*, 294). The quarry is sometimes the grave itself (a symbol of course of moribund social institutions), the bones of Ezekiel's vision "shaking, convuls'd," as even the grave "shrieks with delight" and "swells with wild desire, / And milk & blood & glandous wine" (*The Song of Los*, 7:32, 35, 37–38; *E.*, 69). Traditional psychology is altered to give primacy and beauty to the sense of touch, and even proverbial language abandons its venerable stoicism: "Exuberance is Beauty," "the genitals Beauty," "the lust of the goat is the bounty of God," "the nakedness of woman is the work of God" (*MHH*, 8:23, 25; 10:61, 64; *E.*, 36–38). Old distinctions between body and soul are collapsed: all-pervasive energy is a staminal human power and salvation comes from the "improvement of sensual enjoyment," from whatever the "enlarged & numerous senses" can perceive (*MHH*, plates 11, 14; *E.*, 38, 39).

Though the Blake of revolutionary sexuality appealed greatly to the generation of Marcuse and Allen Ginsberg, he may now sound a bit shrill to our chastened ears. Oothoon seems particularly strident when she volunteers to trap "girls of mild silver, or of furious gold" to help unfreeze her frigid lover, and lie beside them to watch "their wanton play" (*VDA*, 7:24–25: *E.*, 50). The suggestion of catching girls like animals to provide delectation is offensive. But we perhaps should remember that it might take more than one beauty from Leporello's long and varied list to arouse so dismayingly languid a being as Theotormon, inhibited as he is by his inheritance of venerable repressions sanctioned by church, state, and the literary establishment. And in fairness to Blake we must note that revolutionary sexuality is not always a melting fire or a disruptive tempest. Even in this period of raging antinomianism Blake remembers that appetite can be violent and savage and that love needs the tender curb of gentleness. Contemporary revolutions were freeing men only recently "madden'd with slavery" (*The French Revolution*, line 228; *E.*, 296); now they

> May sing in the village, and shout in the harvest, and
> woo in pleasant gardens,
> Their once savage loves, now beaming with knowledge,
> with gentle awe adorned;
> And the saw, and the hammer, the chisel, the pencil, the
> pen, and the instruments
> Of heavenly song sound in the wilds once forbidden.
>
> [lines 229–32; *E.*, 296]

This vision is social and civilized—a creative expression of sexuality which under repression had been aggressive and warlike. It anticipates a later and greater apocalypse of Blake's maturity, when "sweet Science reigns" (*FZ.*, 139: 10; *E.*, 407).

Fallen Sexuality: "Torments of Love and Jealousy"

O Rose thou art sick.
Blake, "The Sick Rose,"
Songs of Experience; *E.*, 23

Luvah and Vala woke & flew up from the Human Heart
Into the Brain.
Blake, *FZ.*, 10:11–12; *E.*, 305

But how did it come about that an act so solemn in its purpose, an act to which nature invites us by so powerful a summons—how did it come about that this act, the greatest, the sweetest and the most innocent of pleasures, has become the chief source of our depravity and bad conduct?
Denis Diderot, *Supplement to Bougainville's "Voyage"* (1964 ed.), 222

A repeated visual motif in Blake's revolutionary art portrays a supine man over whom a woman crouches or hovers, sometimes in a flame, sometimes in a watery wave, sometimes on a battlefield (Plates XIV, XV). Her purpose seems to be to revive or stimulate him, she obviously being the source of life or leadership, while the male is dead, fainting, or otherwise defeated or incompetent. In a somewhat later work, the *Book of Urizen*, though still well within the revolutionary period of the nineties, Blake radically revised this icon (Plate XVI). The female, no longer a dominant, life-bestowing figure, flees from the man, who rounds himself into an inward-driving, self-embracing circle. In this Blakean version of Genesis, Adam (or Los, the poet-figure, the Imagination) is narcissistic, while Eve, "the first female now separate" (in Blake's myth Enitharmon, the consort of the poet) runs away in "perverse and cruel delight" (*Ur.*, 18:10, 19:12; *E.*, 78, 79). The sexual wars have begun, and they will continue in unremitting fury through the rest of Blake's *oeuvre*, for fallen love is now seen as a universal and pervasive, though not a necessary, human condition. That condition long preceded the outbreak of revolutionary energy—it was indeed one cause of the outbreak. The tragedy Blake now laments is that the revolutionary actors have themselves succumbed to both established perversions and natural perversi-

PLATE XIV. William Blake, Title page of *America,* copy F.

117

PLATE XV. William Blake, Detail of *Europe,* plate 4, copy D.

PLATE XVI. William Blake, *The Book of Urizen*, plate 19, copy G.

ties, and it is therefore fated that only out of such melancholy decline and entrapment can salvation come.

Blake's unforgettably vivid portrayal of the ruined universe, including the fallen palace of once golden love, has been much studied, and we need to recapitulate only the salient features. Female leadership has now become the tyrannous Female Will, a trap baited by sexual attractiveness, while the marriage bed of mutual delight is now frozen and marriage itself an unnatural yoking of youth and age or of otherwise unloving pairs—back to back as on the frontispiece of the *Visions of the Daughters of Albion,* a grotesque, even impossible, coupling reminiscent of the seventh of Goya's grim *Matrimonial Disparate,* in which the marriage union is emblematized by a Siamese-twin-like yoking of man's and woman's hinder parts.

Social disease is perhaps the least of love's afflictions, those of the mind, body, and character operating together being much worse—cruelty, sadism, masochism, nymphomania, phallic violence, castration, erotic delusion. The narcissistic sins Milton foresaw as a result of the Fall are rampant: incest (see Blake's portrayals of Lot and his daughters and of the drunken Noah), the *vice solitaire,* various types of homosexual linkings, and oral-anal copulation. Institutions poison and are poisoned: churches, which bind men's natural longings with cruel briars, themselves embody sexual mysteries and cultic inversions; men drunk with sexual frustration reel off to war; and within the family occur oedipal murders and the life-denying frustrations of tyranny and selfishness. We do not have to await the twentieth century to have unveiled for us the horrors of sexual tortuosity. Blake's version appears in the faintly drawn, sometimes partially erased designs on the pages of the *Four Zoas* manuscript in the British Museum; these are not to be regarded as "high porn" but as an indictment of what body has done to body, mind to body, and body to mind in the Waste Land of Experience.

Professor Damrosch says that Blake came to believe that the torments of love and jealousy arose not as "the misuse of desire only" but because of its "essential nature" (*Symbol,* 212). I do not think that this version of the doctrine of Original Sin—that there is a bent to evil present even in our reproductive life—ever compelled Blake's intellectual allegiance, nor do I believe he ever positioned himself, like a primitive Christian, "to soar away from the vile body" (*Symbol,* 217). In Blake's reworking of Genesis, he departs from the tradition that lust caused the Fall, in part accepted by Milton; instead of blaming libido, he blames the self and a drive toward tyranny, a desire to become a one and only, to expel the other, to create a self-loving narcissistic isolation that is "unprolific," "clos'd," and "unknown" (*Ur.,* 3:2, 24; *E.,* 70, 71). Obsessively repeated, *unknown* suggests being self-closed, solipsistic, no one's object of knowledge. Urizen's darkness is "ninefold" (*Ur.,* 3:9; *E.,* 70), a multiple of Blake's sexual number three, but the meaning is not that he has fallen because of sex but that his selfish singleness has no more need of it: it therefore becomes darkly and perversely absent. And woman is separated from man because the imagination, instead of being revolted and outraged by such onanistic singlehood, feels pity and so dissipates at once the revolutionary anger that could have been redemptive.

From this new female emotion that now enters the psyche and human culture arise all the dreary rituals of institutional pity, and one finds an explanation for the charity, the dole, and the beggary portrayed in the *Songs of Experience* and the Lambeth prophecies. From pity also arises all the false modesty of reluctant, self-effacing, life-denying courtship and coyness that finally causes the hungry male-pursuer and the desiring but fleeing woman to drop in frustrated exhaustion. Honest desire does not produce the Fall, unprolific selfishness does; and the state of the lapséd soul is ratified in pitiful timidity and withdrawal. Blake never relinquished the idea that what poisoned sexuality was not the body itself, desire per se, but debilitations of mind and spirit coming from psychological and institutional tyranny. A starved mind does of course affect the body, for Blake moves from *psyche* to *soma*; and when Albion in *Jerusalem* describes his own pathetic sexual performance in fallen Babylon, he should be regarded as an effect not a cause:

> O how I tremble! how my members pour down milky fear!
> A dewy garment coves me all over, all manhood is gone!
> [30:3–4, *E.,* 176]

Manhood was, however, very much present in Great Eternity, and Blake's accounts of the fallen condition keep invoking that prelapsarian condition as healthy—as if to show us that desire itself is healthy and not a twist in our nature that produced the erotic woes I have catalogued. What Blake called variously "times of old," "Ancient Time," "the once glorious heaven" (*FZ.,* 30:48, 72:38; *Jer.,* 97:2; *E.,* 256, 320, 349) is not merely childhood, innocence, lack of self-consciousness, naturalness. It is to be placed in *illo tempore,* the traditional mythic time of pastoral, Edenic, integrative bliss, to which Blake directs our gaze for our own healing and salvation. Then and there men and women in a sophisticated play of the mind and the body enjoyed communion in an environment of art, science, and culture. On the physical side the *illud tempus* possessed the joys of embracing, insemination, pregnancy, lactation, procreation. Urizen (the mind, the total intellect, reason) partook fully of these joys, his "lap full of seed" and his "hand full of generous fire"

(*Book of Ahania*, 5:29–30; *E.*, 89). Blake's recurring reminders of those happy days even when he is presenting his horrendous portrayal of fallen love is surely an indication that he does not want the betrayal of libidinal power to damn the power itself. Judas should not be allowed to impugn Christ.

But it is not the purpose of this part of the chapter to present the ideal or to allow it to obscure the hideousness of the perverted and the corrupt. I have said that *golden* is an adjective Blake used frequently of erotic love: consider the following defilement of the golden temple by the ejaculation of a diseased phallus—a kind of cultural universalization of the seminal poison of Swift's Baron Cutts the Salamander—

> I saw a chapel all of gold
> That none did dare to enter in
> And many weeping stood without
> Weeping mourning worshipping
>
> I saw a serpent rise between
> The white pillars of the door
> And he forcd & forcd & forcd
> Down the golden hinges tore
>
> And along the pavement sweet
> Set with pearls & rubies bright
> All his slimy length he drew
> Till upon the altar white
>
> Vomiting his poison out
> On the bread & on the wine
> So I turnd into a sty
> And laid me down among the swine.
> [from Blake's Notebook; *E.*, 467–68]

To receive the full force of this poem it is necessary to observe that the golden chapel, before the phallic, serpentine defilement, is closed and barred, with all entrance forbidden. That first perversion (a place of beauty and delight turned by exclusion into a place of "Weeping mourning worshipping") preceded the second and more disgusting one (the extrusion of poison on what once had been the bread and wine of a naturally sacramental union).

Blake's Beulah: Love as Pleasure

Sexual love . . . is the door through which most of us enter the imaginative world, and for many it affords the sole glimpse into that world.

Northrop Frye, *Fearful Symmetry* (1947, 1958), 73

122

William Blake: "Arrows of Desire" and "Chariots of Fire"

There is from great Eternity a mild & pleasant rest
Namd Beulah a Soft Moony Universe feminine lovely
Pure mild & Gentle, given in Mercy to those who sleep
Eternally. Created by the Lamb of God around
On all sides within & without the Universal Man.

Blake, FZ., 5:29–33; E., 303

A popular American gospel song invokes "Beulah Land, sweet Beulah Land," and here and there in rural North America there are small towns that bear this name. One surmises that the song confuses Beulah with heaven and that the place-name confuses it with the Promised Land of Canaan, flowing with milk, honey, and hope. Blake's Beulah is infinitely more complex and meaningful. He derives his concept ultimately from Isaiah 62:4–5, where the prophet promises to Israel a happy marital union with God in a land that is also said to be "married." Bunyan's "Country of *Beulah*" in *Pilgrim's Progress,* whose "Air was very sweet and pleasant," lies on the borders of heaven, within sight of the New Jerusalem, from which, however, it is separated by the river of death. When Pilgrim reaches Beulah, he is almost at the end of his journey, but the river must be traversed as a last obstacle before complete salvation has been achieved. Beulah is a sunny land, beyond the reach of despair and doubt, though the sight of the Celestial City can cause travelers like Christian and Hopeful to fall ill of desire. Beulah heals and comforts them, for it is a place where Christ the King has walked and which he has established; and it has delicious orchards, vineyards, and gardens. Blake's Beulah retains intact much of the symbolism of Bunyan's—with this important difference. The poet has made this place of rest, refreshment, and pleasure a nightscape, lit only by a mild and tender moon. That lesser light enforces Blake's central intention, which is that Beulah should signify romantic love and sexuality.

The importance of a place of rest for Blake's spirit cannot be overstressed. The revolutionary period had taken its toll in "Nervous Fear" produced by "dark horrors" (letter to Flaxman, Sept. 1800; E., 708): and like Bunyan's Christian, Blake and his Los, another Pilgrim of Eternity, had traveled much through "Perils & Darkness" (letter to Butts, 22 Nov. 1802; E., 720). And of course the hideous nadir to which love between the sexes had fallen in the Urizenic and Satanic dispensations must have often led to spectral despair about love and a desire to banish it from the prophetic enterprise:

> Let us agree to give up Love
> And root up the infernal grove

123

Then shall we return & see
The worlds of happy Eternity.
["My Spectre," lines 49–52; *E.*, 477]

The wild beast of a specter, the "insane & most / Deformd" (*FZ.*,
5:38–39; *E.*, 303) part of man, speaks here, and though he may reflect
a Blakean mood, he does not express a permanent Blakean philosophy,
which had no intention ever of giving up love and appropriate sexuality
and which came to recognize that one cannot achieve happy eternity
tout court by rushing into it from the fallen world. Nor can one sustain
for long the Edenic mental struggle of rooting up the Satanic wilder-
ness without a change of imaginative venue that provides calm and rest-
ful pleasure.

Blake's Beulah is a mental creation that followed the sufferings of
his revolutionary period and that grew out of what he called in *Jerusalem* his "three years slumber on the banks of the Ocean" (*Jer.*, plate 3;
E., 145), where he lived in lovely Felpham under the patronage of William
Hayley, a man of liberal, avant-garde sentiments but not of poetic genius,
though he tried hard. In one of his great visions by the oceanside, Blake's
spiritual eyes "expand / . . . Into regions of fire, / Remote from desire"
[he is momentarily in Eden]; but then in the same moment of inspiration he looked earthward

And Saw Felpham sweet
Beneath my bright feet
In soft Female charms
And in her fair arms
My Shadow I knew.
[letter to Butts, 2 Oct. 1800; *E.*, 712–13]

Without using the term *Beulah* Blake in an important autobiographical-
mythological revelation has given us its structure, location, and
dynamics—a moment of intense vision in brilliant light is followed by
a soft and relaxing marital intimacy: first Eden, then Beulah. Sometimes
the sexual embrace induces not the comfort of the uxorial nest but of
innocence or childhood:

The honey of her Infant lips
The bread & wine of her sweet smile
The wild game of her roving Eye
Does him to infancy beguile.
["The Mental Traveller," lines 69–72; *E.*, 485]

A return to innocence can be either blessedly fructifying or arrestingly
regressive—a paradox that endows the Beulah-embrace with strongly
divergent alternative possibilities.

Such possibilities remain present in Blake's own etiological analysis of his Beulah-concept in Western culture during the Christian era. That lovely but difficult Lambeth prophecy entitled *Europe,* which begins by saluting the joys of touch and so alerting us to expect the theme of sexuality in the main part of the work, presents the course of the Christian centuries as a woman's dream, in which energy is repressed and the sexual life flickers into flame in moments of bliss that are temporally just that—sudden, brief, and secret moments. Yet within that long dispensation in which virginity is exalted and modesty cultivated, there are adumbrations of richer pleasures, and these are imagistically expressed in the poem by means of: "the gay fishes on the wave," "lovely eagles" with "golden wings," "the many colour'd bow," the "Soft soul of flowers," the "crystal house," and "the lineaments of gratified desire" (13:14; 14:3, 7–8, 10, 11, 19; *E.,* 65–66). All these points of troped intensity add up to the later Beulah, which we can now see Blake has in part distilled from woman's admittedly ambivalent role in the otherwise largely male-oriented and male-directed culture which he as a Western Christian had inherited.

Blake came to feel that these all-too infrequent and disparate moments of golden pleasure needed to be hypostasized as a more permanent resource within individual and corporate culture, and we see that the great sexual myth of *Vala, Milton,* and *Jerusalem,* which he developed during and after his period of rural retreat, takes up all the hints we have mentioned so far and, making them richer and subtler than they had been, organizes them into a structure. Beulah sometimes looks like a winter hibernation, a place of sleep and protection from surrounding storms. Though it is a place for men, its décor, its appointments, become in time insistently feminine. It is in fact feminine space, which man enters for his own and his partner's pleasure. No doubt it took on this quality because Blake was physiologically very much a typical male, and he therefore tended to conceive the place of his own pleasurable expansion and expression as being female, just as he—like male poets all through the course of our history—made his inspiring muse feminine. It would surely have been otherwise had a physiologically typical woman created Beulah, and it will be otherwise as more and more women explore freely the deep recesses of their own desiring selves.

As a completed structure Beulah is regarded as having been created by Christ and as continually being suffused by his protecting, forgiving mildness. Christ is needed here because bodies are needed—sexual, physical bodies, without which there can be neither religion nor art—and Christ in one long tradition and certainly in Blake's own myth is the benign creator. But he is also needed because gentleness is needed.

Sexual appetite without Christian love, Blake came to believe, could become obsessive and devouring, and the return of Christ to Blake's myth in the early years of the nineteenth century bore the profoundest implications for Beulah. It was inevitable ("Because the Lamb of God Creates himself a bride & wife") that "the male & female live the life of Eternity" (FZ., 22:15–16; E., 391); and their conjunction spells Beulah as well as Eden. Albion, who during his long separation from his female consort in his fallen soporific state was alternately licentious and puritanical, at once sexist and sexual, comes at length, under the ministrations of the lovely Christ-like Jerusalem, to see that "Love & Pity are the same; a soft repose! / Inward complacency [that is, shared pleasure] of Soul: a Self-annihilation!" (Jer., 23:14–15; E., 168). Christ has indeed transformed love into something Beulah-like—in its mildness and self-sacrificial service.

And yet the Beulah baptized by Christ remains sexual, never slipping into androgynous delicacy or the undifferentiated pleasures of monosexuality. When regarded as a river, or as liquid in motion, Beulah flows on as "mild & liquid pearl" (Milton, 21:15, E., 115)—that is, as both maternal lactation and seminal discharge; and so it flowed also in Great Eternity, in illo tempore, the pre-fallen condition. It is not only Christ who creates and sanctions Beulah; Milton too enters it—to the enormous improvement of his harsh spirit. In the poem Milton, addressed appropriately to the "Daughters of Beulah" (2:1; E., 96), here Blake's own gracious muses, the great Puritan redeems what his wives and daughters had known in part, what he had sorely needed and at least partially rejected—sexual friendships possessing color, beauty, delicacy, and repose. Milton achieves such appropriation of the ewig Weibliche by returning to earth—another Christ, as it were, in a Second Coming—and by embracing a virgin and then engaging in what the poet calls "wondrous . . . acts by me unknown / Except remotely" (40:2–3; E., 141). Paradoxically, we can be less remote about those acts than Blake even though they took place in his own garden. In order to unite with his female emanation Milton must "[condense] all his Fibres" (37:6; E., 137)—fibres being a sexual term and condense suggesting phallic concentration—to which the virgin responds with a dolorous shriek as she unites with her blessed and blessing ravisher. The emotions are comprehensive as well as intense, and the moment of desire is majestic as well as beautiful. But despite the blood and thunder the maiden becomes a dove; and the gentle spirit, who animates her and whom we recognize as the woman Ololon, now descends "as a Moony Ark" (42:7; E., 143)—a Beulah sign. Christ expectedly materializes in order to bless the new Milton of loving tenderness and sexual grace. In a profound way Blake has done to Milton what Dorothy did to Wordsworth—he has softened his precursor's harsh sublimity to gentle beauty. The need for such mildness in love is deeply felt by Blake's persons, especially in their fallen states. Orc as Luvah asks his consort:

> When wilt thou put on the Female Form as in time of old
> With a Garment of Pity & Compassion like the garment of
>   God?
>
> [18:35; *E.*, 112]

The need signaled by that *cri du coeur* is filled by the Christ-infused Beulah, to which men in Eden or in Ulro (Blake's hell) can repair for the restoration of their souls.

Even so, human nature being what it is, Beulah does remain fragile. In that lovely but mysterious poem, "The Crystal Cabinet" (*E.*, 488–89), a maiden catches the poet and locks him in a cabinet made of gold, pearl, and crystal, which opens into "a lovely Moony Night" (the iconic sign of Beulah). The captive warms with desire as he sees another maiden like his attractive captor, but when he remains unsatisfied with mutual kissing and strives to penetrate to the very essence of the place and to seize "its inmost Form / With ardor fierce and hands of flame," he bursts the crystal cabinet and so destroys Beulah as he himself reverts to a weeping childhood. This poem may be describing, very subtly, sexual initiation; but it may also be setting up a contrast between Beulah experience and something much profounder, a contrast to which we shall return.

It should now be clear why Blake has transformed the sun of Bunyan's Beulah into his own Beulah moon, often only a delicate crescent moon at that. As we remember, he had in his revolutionary period called for lustful, open, free love consummated in full daylight. He has now, like an English Novalis, as it were, decided to sing hymns to the night when writing love poetry. "William Bond" (*E.*, 496–98) may in fact present William Blake himself confessing to a radical change in attitude:

> I thought Love livd in the hot sun shine
> But O he lives in the Moony light
> I thought to find Love in the heat of day
> But sweet Love is the Comforter of Night.

The speaker learns that love can begin, unglamorously, in pity and gentle relief of suffering—a point of view that makes the later Blake highly sympathetic in spirit to medieval charity and mildness. Love can and does exist in the winter of our discontent and in the night of suffering and deprivation. If so, we owe its preservation to Beulah.

To get better perspective on Beulah we must go outside Blake's myth and consider other organizations of similar materials. Emanuel Sweden-borg almost regularly saw the various types of love he discriminated in their institutional and conventional relationships. "Conjugial love" (for so the translator insisted on spelling the adjective, following the author's Latin) of course refers to monogamous marriage, to which scor-tatory love is also related though as a hellish antitype of the uxorial heaven. *Pellicacy,* the premarital keeping of one mistress, the Swedish seer places well below sex in marriage though it is above conjoint con-cubinage, a detestable and illicit practice in which a married man keeps a mistress. How unlike this social structuring are the psychological edi-fices of Blake, who in sensing the omnipresence of the body is much closer to Freud than to Swedenborg, though Freud is much more con-cerned with bodily orifices and their psychological equivalents and ef-fects than is Blake. The poet's myth personifies "the nervous system of the vegetated man" as Allamanda, the "male seed" as Antamon, the stomach as Bowlahoola, the womb as Cathedron; and in treating the lower body the poet sometimes achieves comic verve. Beulah is of course the place of genital sexual pleasure, but it is not that alone: it is also the place of maternal love and protection, and sexual desire dwells rather more comfortably in Beulah for not being there alone. Romantic art-ists, Blake among them, loved to create the traditional icons of Charity and her children, and Beulah can in part be regarded as a repository for such delicate and sentimental groupings. We may recall at this point that Coleridge stressed gradations and kinds of love in proximity; if we also remember that he placed these in the family circle, we acquire still another perspective on Blake's Beulah. It is in this combination of vari-ous sorts and conditions of love all united in tender bonds that his Beu-lah becomes the mythological equivalent of the nuclear family.

Why does Blake structure his Beulah as threefold? A very impor-tant reason is that *three* is one—but *only* one—digit less than *four,* the number of Edenic fulfillment and integration; and we shall make much of the fact that threefold Beulah is below, but not far below, fourfold Eternity. Blake's *three* may have come from Milton, who gave to his hell a "thrice threefold" set of gates, brass, iron, and rock, each con-tributing in its turn three, for a total of nine (*Par. Lost,* II, 645–48). But Blake had developed his own hell (Ulro), to which he assigned the num-ber *one* of single uninspired vision, and also his own world of vegetable generation, to which *two* was appropriate because of sexual coupling. He wanted both of these below Beulah, to which he chose to transfer the Miltonic *three* and its multiples, without carrying over the earlier poet's hellish parody of Triune ultimacy but not without recalling his own radically revised hell of energy and creativity. Basic to the threefold of Beulah is the threefold in the constitution of man: the head, the heart, the reins or the loins (see *FZ.*, 100:23–24; *E.*, 373). Each of these parts of man was considered to have in its sexual or threefold center "A Three-fold Atmosphere Sublime continuous from Urthonas world" (*FZ.*, 87:10; *E.*, 368)—that is, these internal Beulahs should be regarded either as contiguous with art or as the creation of the imagination. Since the very center is erotic even though the particular psychological or physiologi-cal zone itself may seem far from that, Blake, reminding us somewhat of Freud's pansexualism, is capable of applying sexually loaded adjec-tives to each center: thus he refers to "the white brain,"* the "red hot heart," and the loins divided into the "two lovely Heavens" of "milky seed"—the testes of course (*Milton,* 19:55–56, 60; *E.*, 113). It would therefore be an error to consider as parallel to Blake's ordering the con-ventional tripartite division of man into body, soul, and spirit or into body, mind, and soul, with stoical implications of higher and lower. Blake's threefold is not Paulinian—those in Christ "walk not after the flesh but after the spirit" (Romans 8:1); in Blake, energy from each realm unites them all and makes the totality a field of interacting forces. To be technically as exact as we possibly can, Blake's three—the mind, the heart, and the sexual organs—do not themselves constitute Beulah, but each provides an entrance into it and also a possible exit from it. What Blake says is essentially this: that to sexual pleasure (that is, to Beulah) there are three possible entrances: from the intellectual, from the sen-timental, from the libidinal itself; and also three possible exits—into the intellectual, into the sentimental, and more deeply (sometimes more dangerously) into the libidinal. This kind of flexible insight, making sexual energy an active force in all departments of life, seems to open up love-pleasures of various kinds to both individual and corporate man and to suggest possible bodily approaches to both individual works of the imagination and cultural movements like rationalism, sentimental-ism, and empiricism. The important point to remember is that Blake's psychology needs a "place" like Beulah, a somatic *and* psychological condition of sexual and related pleasures that cannot be totally iden-tified with any single part of our physical being like the head, the heart, the loins, but that affects and is affected by them all. Beulah is threefold because it looks in these three directions.

This perspective on Beulah permits us to distinguish it, sexual though it is, from the purely procreative, procreation having been traditionally

---

*If this is more than a literal "color" (Blake's rendition of "gray matter"), is it meta-phorical? If so, what is the metaphor? White heat, white purity, or the snowy coolness of rational intelligence? If either of the last two, the sexual meaning would come as an inverse.

considered the chief and sometimes the only justification of sexuality. Though Blake cannot be said always to separate the weaving of bodies, either in creating babies or poems, from Beulah-like situations, he normally used other words for reproduction itself: generation, vegetable nature, stems of vegetation. And Beulah is not intimately associated with looms or forges, with weaving or the working of metal. It is indeed not primarily a place of work at all but of rest. It is sexual pleasure considered for its own sake as play, rest, and refreshment which occupies us when we are in Beulah; we are not primarily concerned with creation, though pleasure affects and is affected by productivity of more than one kind. In Beulah contrarieties do not clash, as in intellectual battle; opposites are true together and simultaneously, as they are in the Freudian dream, without negatives or oxymoronic antitheses.

Beulah is a place of pleasure and rest for the body, of dreams in the body, of joys induced by the body. That central truth must never be forgotten. It almost was, by Albion, who had been so brain-washed by laws of Urizenic and Satanic chastity and asceticism, that he became almost amusingly reluctant to accept his own redemption:

> The Eternal Man also sat down upon the Couches of Beulah
> Sorrowful that he could not put off his new risen body
> In mental flames the flames refusd they drove him back
>   to Beulah
> His body was redeemed to be permanent thro the Mercy
>   Divine
>
> [*FZ.*, 125:36–39; *E.*, 395]

Blake's flaming mental energies like and respect Beulah and the body, and they actively insist upon both as necessary for salvation. Milton, "revised" by Blake into a person who has come to accept the body and who is therefore much less reluctant than the hesitant Albion, willingly embraces his female in "wondrous . . . acts" (*Milton*, 40:2; *E.*, 141) and demonstrates that just as revolutionary political acts were conceived by the Blake of the 1790s to commence in sexual union, so mental revolution is now also conceived of as beginning in physical "Embraces" and "Cominglings: from the Head even to the Feet" (*Jer.*, 69:43; *E.*, 223). Beulah has become an eternal principle.

Beulah and Eden: Sexual Love in Integrated Humanity

> *Humanity knows not of Sex: Wherefore are sexes in Beulah?*
>
> Blake, *Jerusalem*, 44:33; *E.*, 193

William Blake: "Arrows of Desire" and "Chariots of Fire"

[Christ's] Maternal Humanity must be put off Eternally
Lest the Sexual Generation swallow up Regeneration
Blake, Jerusalem, 90:36; E., 250

> When weary Man enters his Cave
> He meets his Saviour in the Grave
> Some find a Female Garment there
> And some a Male, woven with care
> Lest the Sexual Garments sweet
> Should grow a devouring Winding sheet.
>
> Blake, For the Sexes:
The Keys of the Gates, 21, 26; E., 268

Art can never exist without Naked Beauty displayed.
Blake, The Laocoön (E., 275)

O holy Generation! [Image] of regeneration!
Jer., 7:65; E., 150

If Blake's central meanings can rightly be thought to reside in his myth and if that myth has so far been correctly interpreted, it may occasion some surprise that so many scholarly critics, particularly more recent ones, have found the poet's treatment of sexual love to reveal reservation, distrust, even dismay. Why is this so? There are doubtless some who are constitutionally disposed, perhaps by the bent of our age toward grim and unrelenting realism, to censure the better (in this case Beulah) for not being the best (Eden). (I might interrupt to say that Blake honors Beulah precisely because it is not—and should not be—the highest or intensest kind of experience humankind is capable of.) Others may not have taken into sufficient account the truth that Blake's richest ideas almost always bear the seeds of paradox in them and that it would be unusual if so central a motif as erotic love should have been exempted from his typically oxymoronic vision. Everyone must surely acknowledge the two-edged, potentially contradictory nature of such symbols as the following: fire which can purify and fire which can destroy; pity which can spring up like a fresh spring in Innocence and pity which can ooze out in piously hypocritical utterance as we "make somebody Poor" ("The Human Abstract," E., 27), in the world of Experience; the cruciform position which is assumed by the Christ of forgiving love and also by Urizen or by the villainous Hand in Jerusalem. Recognizing the marvellously enriching qualities that reside in imaginative contraries, we do well, however, not to invoke ambivalence, ambiguity,* or the fash-

---

*I have myself used the word ambiguity of aspects of Blake's responses to sexuality,

131

ionable "undecidability" too quickly—before we have attempted to disclose the energy of the paradox, an energy which is released fully only when we discover what element in it should be given priority or privilege. And in the matter of sexual love, the dynamic of the myth tells us that ultimately the positive side of Beulah can and does win out over the libidinal terrors of perverted generation. Considerable inconvenience arises when we make a Manichaean out of Blake, exalting the evil that exists in compellingly vivid presentation into a principle coeval with the good. But the chief reason, I believe, why Blakean physicality in love has been denigrated is that Blake himself, outside his myth and sometimes even within it, has seemed himself to denigrate it in memorable aphoristic utterances, some of them given as epigraphs to this section. Let us now try to determine whether these and similar apothegms are uttered in a dramatic context or are otherwise to be qualified. And surely Blake must be accorded the right of a lyric poet to express a mood often contrary to the drift of his main philosophical meaning. Many a cry of despair and disgust, like many of his dismissive gnomic sentences, must have been born of personal sexual suffering.

Like Paul the Apostle, Blake was frequently pricked by the thorn in his flesh and was capable of expressing ideas that sound like ascetic anticorporality. Commenting on one of his own paintings, Blake says: "in Paradise they have no Corporeal Body that originated with the Fall & was calld Death" (*A Vision of the Last Judgment, E.,* 564). (It needs to be said that Blake's prose-comments on his own and others' work, valuable and vivid though these can be, often need the qualification provided by the main meanings of his myth.) Another of these expressions of anticorporality has been abbreviated to read, "spiritual Hate, from which Springs Sexual Love," by a commentator who calls it a "perception," and compares it to our own contemporary Robert Stoller's recent thesis that hostility, the hidden or open wish to harm another, produces and enhances sexual instinct and arousal. But the context in *Jerusalem* (54:12, *E.,* 203) shows that Albion is here in the grip of his own specter, his psychic deformation, and that he is suffering from parental jealousy at seeing his sons under the spell of the fallen Luvah—a bondage which the father sees as "spiritual Hate, from which springs"—not sexual love per se but "Sexual Love as iron chains." Should

but I object when it is applied too freely to important antithetical and contrastive structures or when it is used to suggest a radical kind of inherent evil or mischief that obscures the ultimate optimism of the thought. Thus Damrosch says of Beulah that it is "the feminized paradise which Blake regarded with deep suspicion" (*Symbol,* 183). He also says of the sexuality of Generation that it is "filled—one might say pregnant—with ambiguity" (190, n.73). Other examples could be cited if space permitted.

the emotions of a fallen man among the ruins of his world be considered finally normative?

When Los in a moment of distress says, "Humanity knows not of Sex," he goes on to ask, "wherefore are Sexes in Beulah?" and then gives a richly allusive image of the sex act:

> In Beulah the Female lets down her beautiful Tabernacle;
> Which the Male enters magnificent between her Cherubim
> And becomes One with her.
>
> [*Jer.*, 44:34–36; *E.*, 193]

This may well be, as it has been called, "the sacred rites of sexual Religion"—from the point of view of Eden a "ritual of guilt . . . rather than the delight of joy." If so, Blake was using the religious parallel to parody both priestly and amorous pomposity—and he did that frequently. But even in Blake's bitterest moments he points out or implies an optimistic alternative, which should be considered as possible even here. The couple are presented as "condensing in Self-love / The Rocky law of Condemnation" (lines 36–37); and since Los appears here with the "Divine Vision" (line 19), it is at least possible that in the very selfishness of sexual pleasure (and Blake was not sentimental about *that*!) the Lord of Mercy is helping to create a body or some kind of materiality for error so that it can be cast out in a Last Judgment by love or art. The passage then goes on to present the loins as the place of ultimate salvation, even though the route is indirect. And we do well to remember that, as W.J.T. Mitchell has pointed out, Blake in the famous representation of the awakening of humanity in *Albion Rose* has shifted the center of gravity from the navel, its traditional place in Renaissance art, to the loins.

The truth is that Beulah does open toward both earth and eternity, that it is located between our globe and Eden, contiguous with both. Its geography declares that sexuality can drive toward "poisonous stupor & deadly intoxication" (*Jer.*, 38:29; *E.*, 185) but that it is also a "translucence" (*Jer.*, 87:11; *E.*, 246)—that is, a window that lets in prophetic light. If Beulah did not open into the vegetated world, sexuality as we know it could not possibly exist, and Blake always wanted to retain essential human physical structures despite the devastations wrought by the Fall. Not being a Docetist or a Buddhist or a Hindu mystic but a Christian who believed in the resurrection of the body, he has the imaginative faculty in man admire the "translucent Wonder" of the human body with its "bright loins" (*Jer.*, 14:17, 19; *E.*, 158) not only because it can lead to vision but also because its "golden gate . . . opens into the vegetative world" (line 20). I have no wish that we forget the soul-searing sufferings that the mortal body can produce, but it is important never to lose sight of these positive qualities in corporality, which I judge ought to take precedence over the negative, over lapses from or perversions of a clearly ideal potential. One scholar has found something "amiss" being recorded in the following lines:

> When those who disregard all Mortal Things saw a
> Mighty-One
> Among the Flowers of Beulah still retain his awful
> strength
> They wonderd, checking their wild flames.
> [*Jer.*, 55:1–3; *E.*, 204]

But why "amiss"? If Beulah is regarded with grudgingly, Paulinian reservations as only a kind of comfort station, it might indeed be "disturbed by the appearance of such a majestic being." But, as we have seen, Beulah is also a place of sexual energy and renewal, and what the Eternals see here is nothing less than the return of Christ without loss of strength to what he has himself created. If so, the Eternals, who are far from being statically infallible, are being taught a lesson we all should learn about Blake's respect for the "Staminal Virtues of Humanity" (Annotations to Lavater, *E.*, 601): they are embodied in Beulah and can fructify and energize life.

Much has been made of the fact that Blake often alludes to Christ's denial in the Gospels that the institution of marriage exists in heaven. The most forthright of these allusions, "In Eternity they neither marry nor are given in marriage" (*Jer.*, 30:15; *E.*, 176), is, however, the judgment not of Blake or Christ but of fallen Albion uttering derivative orthodox doctrine in a state of pain. But Los-Blake speaking as a *raisonneur* does say to his consort: "'Sexes must vanish & cease / To be, when Albion arises from his dead repose" (92:13–14; *E.*, 252); and Jerusalem, Blake's Mary, says to Vala, his Venus, in a period of distress: "Humanity is far above / Sexual organization, & the visions of the night of Beulah / Where Sexes wander in dreams of bliss" (79:73–75; *E.*, 236). The context of each of these last two statements shows it to be dramatic. In the first the poet is comforting his wife, who sees her sexual-poetic labors coming to an end, and in the second the personification of the eternal feminine of gentleness and kindness (Jerusalem) is rebuking her earthly counterpart (Vala) for engaging in a cruel and devouring type of sexuality and in the process underrating or neglecting the bliss of the mysterious, nightlike qualities of the sexual Beulah, dragging it out into the light of the day, as indeed Blake himself had done in his Orcan period.

And yet Blake in his myth does make Eden the place of thought and mental creation and Beulah the place of sexual refreshment. Why the clear separation of these adjoining entities even though they often interact and even interpenetrate? He could easily have created one mythic place, as D.H. Lawrence would surely have done, where the prophetic and the erotic ecstasies would unite. Once again, we must consult the myth itself and not isolated, dramatic apothegms to arrive at the full meaning. If we look closely at the language used in the greatest of the apocalyptic climaxes, we find that sexual metaphors seem to imply the presence of some kind of sexual energy in the place of the highest fulfillment. There the senses continue to expand and contract; there "Embraces are Cominglings: from the Head even to the Feet" (69:43; E., 223), with the suggestion that something more totally conjunctive than genital union is envisaged, though this last is either included or recollected. Eden is, to be sure, characterized more by the clash of contraries in creation than by any kind of embrace, but even in the wars of intellect (which we must note are also wars of "mutual Benevolence," "Wars of Love") the bow that is used to shoot the Arrows of Love is "Male & Female" and is grasped firmly "between the Male & Female loves" (97:12–15; E., 256). This troping takes into account both sexes but also implies that in order to get maximum resilience, force, and balance for the shot, you must not favor one sexual side or the other. The fourfold man still has "the Human Nerves of Sensation," which exist in "Rivers of bliss"; the "Expansive Nostrils" show that the senses are still flexible; the "Nervous fibres" (those sexual words again) can still vibrate with energy. Each of the chariots of the Almighty, which bear the fourfold, fully integrated man, is a "Sexual Threefold," by which image Blake is re-asserting the presence of the body in Great Eternity (98:11–38; E., 258–59). As Northrop Frye has said, "The chariot is actually the vehicular form of the driver himself, or his own body."

Now if this is true, if we can indeed trust the metaphors when they seem to imply the impregnation of intellectual eternity with Beulah sexuality, we have to repeat our question: why the mythic separation of the two realms? In the conclusion of the greatest apocalyptic climax, that of *Jerusalem,* Blake's "Human Forms identified" and returned "wearied / Into the Planetary lives of Years Months Days & Hours reposing / And then Awaking into his Bosom in the Life of Immortality" (99:1–4; E., 258). That return is of course a return to Beulah, and the absolute necessity of the rest it provides is measured by the corresponding intensity of Eden. The moment and place of fiery prophecy is not also the moment and place to indulge fiery sexual desire. Blake makes, it seems to me, a sensible separation, one that the experience of men of genius and power would seem to ratify. People

whose energies are low may have known this truth all along and wonder
what the fuss has been about. But Blake did *not* know it all along, and
one reason for the insistence upon separate realms was a profound need
for sexual rest and sexual gentleness in the poet's own psyche. Romantics, perhaps because of their own intense experiences, are more realistic than they are often credited with being. Blake was not tempted to
make sexual pleasure either summit or essence. In what may have been
his last word on sexuality, he put it in its place, so to speak. Calling
it a multi-colored, multi-functional, and beautiful veil that enfolds the
world, he said:

> Sometimes it shall assimilate with mighty Golgonooza:
> Touching its summits: & sometimes divided roll apart.
> As a beautiful Veil so these Females shall fold & unfold
> According to their will the outside surface of the Earth
> An outside shadowy Surface superadded to the real
>   Surface;
> Which is unchangeable for ever & ever Amen: so be it!
>
> [83:43–48; *E.*, 242]

Blake elsewhere could be both more censorious and also more encomi-
astic of sexuality. But the last Amen of the quotation accepts and blesses
it. It may not be more than a shadowy surface when compared to hard
matter, but it rests upon durable reality; and it can sometimes attain
the very pinnacles of the city of art.

Anne Mellor must surely represent a growing body of contemporary
thought about Blake when she says that he habitually equates woman
with either "the subordinate or the perversely dominant." It is not difficult to see that much in Blake's language would seem to reveal blind
insensitivity to those now engaged in one of the most fruitful enterprises
of our day, the opening of our mental eyes to the pervasive presence
and mischief of sexual stereotypes. I think we must concede that in
these matters Blake's sight was indeed partially "fogged," though, I would
hasten to add, less so than that of most earlier poets. It is inevitable
that a pre-revolutionary thinker, however prophetic his vision, will perceive differently from those whose consciousness has already been raised
historically. It must be also inevitable, though the point is currently being made with tiresome iteration, that as a man he will in the nature
of things conceive of woman differently from a member of his own sex.
Beulah is eroticized feminine space because its creator was a man, just
as a woman's Beulah is likely to be eroticized male expansiveness.

But Eternity, though it may often recall, embody, or be energized by
sexual bliss, need not be conceived of in the same way, for it is a place
of imaginative possibility; and the real test of the tolerance and com-

prehensiveness of Blake's thought is not how he structures the place of nocturnal fantasy and delight but whom he admits to the place of mental creation and production. Well before he had refined and ripened his concept of Eden, he had launched the careers of several women—Thel, Ona, Lyca, Oothoon—whose seeking and acting we have earlier glanced at. If these women fail, they fail less because their characters are fated to be weak and submissive than because they encounter social resistance that is superhumanly powerful, frightening, or beguiling. In Blake's later myth it would be well to ask if Enitharmon, Vala, Ololon, and Jerusalem can be regarded, fallen or unfallen, as only attributes of man or as weak derivations or reflections of his powers. Enitharmon can be shy, modest, frightened, deceitful, but she can also be resistant, reproachful, wilful, fully individualistic, an eloquent defender of her own rights. And of course she can achieve the status of a creative imaginative collaborator. Vala can be as tyrannical as Urizen and as alluring as Venus, but she cannot be called a cipher or anybody's pale reflection and is, all in all, a dismayingly real, alluring, and assertive presence. Ololon's venturing forth from great Eternity can be paralleled in majesty only by Christ's descent to earth and Milton's return to it. Hers is a freely willed quest for being, recognition, and permanence that opens a wide road to eternity.

Can woman herself traverse that road and enter the place of fourfold integration? Or is Eden for men only? Ololon claims her right to be there. She asks Milton, "Are we Contraries, O Milton, Thou & I?" and the implied answer is yes—that she as well as he deserves that honorific term, a qualification for mental fight. She talks of "*Our* Human Power" which "can sustain the severe contentions / Of Friendship," though, like Blake her creator, she properly wishes such friendship separated from sexual arousal (*Milton,* 41:32–35; *E.,* 143). There is no doubt that when she descends to Blake's neighborhood she burns with the fires of intellect that "rejoic'd in Felphams Vale" (42:9; *E.,* 143). Milton himself had defined eternity as a place of contraries; and Blake, who in one of his greatest imaginative efforts added to that lofty and strenuous condition qualities that are human, tender, and even feminine, could surely not confine his relations with women only to the soft embraces of Beulah.

Blake has some difficulty in dramatizing and humanizing his Christ, for all his belief in the humanity of the Savior; and what Alicia Ostriker rightly says of Jerusalem is true of Jesus as well: he "simply is." Action, protest, argument are usually undertaken by his surrogates or types. It is true that Blake says that in Eternity woman "has no Will of her own" (*Last Judgment, E.,* 562). But if woman is denied will in Eternity, we should remember that under the Covenant of Forgiveness the new and gentle Jehovah also lacks will, a fallen, depraved quality given to Vala and Urizen and to the tyrannical patriarchs of the Hebrew-Christian code. Will tends to be absent from the state of highest fulfillment: other qualities and other quests and a different orientation toward the self make it irrelevant or obtrusive. So it is no loss that Jerusalem in particular and idealized women in general lack it. In that respect they are like Blake's redeemed father-figure, who was once all will and power but has finally transcended that condition.

Such are the exigencies of Blake's kind of art that woman in her highest state is, like Christ, rather an icon than a real character. So Jerusalem appears first as a persecuted charity figure like the medieval Jane Shore, whom Blake had long loved, then as the bride of Christ, then as liberty in every human being, but most fully as Eve-Mary, the mother of us all, an entire human being with a complete endowment of mind, heart, and loins. Her head, with its gates of pearl, reflect Eternity and suggest that, like Ololon, she is accorded a presence in Eden. Her bosom is beautiful (white, translucent) but also "sublime," for she is "Terrible to behold" in her "extreme beauty and perfection" (*Jer.*, 86:14–16; *E.*, 244). It is through bosoms, as Robert Gleckner has seen, that one human being enters another's humanity and art, and Blake gives to Jerusalem's bosom the Burkean and Kantian qualities of both beauty (traditionally considered feminine) and sublimity (traditionally considered male). Finally, her loins, covered with wings that both reveal and hide, burn with flames of holiness that are twelvefold, a multiple of both three (the sexual) and four (the integrative and the imaginative). It would have been instructive had Blake possessed a novelist's power and been able to give us a life-like rendition of his ideal woman in a realistic narrative action. But Blake does what he does, and it would be difficult to think of an icon that embodies more human range, variety, and dignity— from sexual competence to imaginative élan—than this emblem of integrated humanity whose sex happens to be feminine. (See Plate XVIII.)

Jerusalem is of course exceptional, as indeed Christ and Milton are, which in no way weakens their exemplary power. Yet we should continue to ask whether women *in general* are regarded as lacking the energy of a creative contrary. Do they normally belong only in Beulah and Generation or can they too achieve a place high in humanity? We must always bear in mind that Blake uses the terms *man, humanity, mankind* generically for *homo* and does not identify any of them with *vir*, individual man or man the gender-differentiated sexual being. Blake, it is true, does not pause to make points about gender in his vocabulary and grammar, as we do in our day of heightened linguistic awareness.

His fullest statement of how human beings of whatever sex unite in Eden must be analyzed, for it makes clear that "When souls mingle & join through all the fibres of brotherhood," he might just as well have used the word *sisterhood* or *manhood*. *Fibres,* as we have seen, implies sexuality, reminding us once more that Beulah is not far away. The passage is also important for it shows that that somewhat unfortunate word *emanation,* which to us certainly implies inferiority and was often used of woman alone, must also be conceived of entirely apart from gender, in a context where distinct and clearly differentiated sexes are present as equals:

> When in Eternity Man [*homo,* the generic term] converses with
>   Man [also humanity] they enter
> Into each other's Bosom (which are Universes of delight)
>   [both the words *bosom* and *delight* imply the
>   presence of the two sexes]
> In mutual interchange. and first their Emanations meet
> Surrounded by their Children.
>   [Here the human analogy is extended from couples to
>   families, suggesting that a full Beulah experience
>   lies behind the Edenic experience, one that
>   involves parental-filial as well as sexual love]
>   if they embrace & comingle
> The Human Four-fold Forms mingle also in thunders of Intellect
>   [The passage would be meaningless if women and
>   children were in a lower world mingling all by
>   themselves, while men only mingled in the higher
>   sphere.]
> But if the Emanations [male and female] mingle not with
>   storms & agitations
> Of earthquakes & consuming fires they roll apart in fear
>   [such separation in Blake is usual between the
>   sexes in a fallen state]
> For Man cannot unite with Man but by their Emanations
> Which stand both Male & Female at the gates of each Humanity.

Blake could scarcely be clearer without ceasing to be Blake: emanations are not derivative female beings dependent on the male but are male *and* female aspects of humanity, which, because of their associations with Beulah, are a means of producing and supporting by primary sexuality a higher though secondary union of person (male or female) with person (female or male). But I must complete quoting the passage, which is too often truncated in quotation, especially because it uses a bold word which at first blush seems to contradict what has been here asserted. Having described the unions of eternity, Los then comes firmly back to earth and requests a sexual intimacy with his wife:

> How then can I ever again be united as Man with Man
>   [the *as* is important, suggesting the generic idea of
>   human being, not an exclusive male world; that kind of
>   higher union he has ultimately in mind for himself and
>   his consort]
> While thou my Emanation refusest my Fibres of dominion
>   [she is his emanation as he is hers; *fibres* must here
>   refer to the male semen; *dominion* does not suggest
>   Urizenic tyranny but the primacy and necessity of male
>   insemination for usual human pleasure and for generation]
> When Souls mingle & join thro all the Fibres of Brotherhood
> Can there be any secret joy on earth greater than this?
>
> [*Jer.,* 88:3–15; *E.,* 246]

The last couplet could serve as a summary not only of this section on the position of woman but of the whole chapter, for *fibres, secret,* and *joy* bring a sexual metaphor into Eden, showing the absolute necessity of Beulah as an inspiration and support of fourfold humanity. Stated more simply, even baldly, Los-Blake asks first for a sexual liaison with his wife as a prelude to an even more intense intellectual and artistic collaboration. The whole passage, which I have broken into so ungraciously for purposes of analysis, gives the true meaning of *emanation* (the true complementary, cooperating opposite of either sex). Blake did break away from the prison of his own sex long enough to define and envision an intersexual world of intense mutuality and equality.

Everything I have said so far about Innocence, Experience, Generation, Beulah, "Ancient Times" (the *illud tempus*), Great Eternity, and Eden should have shown us that for Blake androgyny was at most an implied general metaphor for union and not an ideal suggesting the reduction or elimination of sexual difference. For in all the realms I have mentioned, highly distinct sexual bodies energetically desire each other, either literally or metaphorically, and we should remember that strongly heterosexual tropes would not be used by a great poet if he intended a bland, desire-free world of more or less sexless beings contemplating higher things or of beings so circumscribed that longing was entirely inner and subjective, one internal part vibrating in response to another internal part. Such indoor circuitry is not Blakean. Blake was Christian, not Platonic. When he said, "I know of no other Christianity and of no other Gospel than the liberty *both of body & mind* to exercise the divine Arts of Imagination" (*Jer.,* 77; *E.,* 231; emphasis added), we are not to think of the body as possessing anything other than understandably and normally human desires and powers.

Blake never used the term *androgyne* in nominal or adjectival form, except in conversation, when the word *androgynous* threw Crabb Robinson into a state of irremediable confusion. But he did use the term *her-maphrodite* many times, always in the most pejorative sense conceivable. For example, he gathers all the enemies of Jesus into a Satanic hermaphrodite, a symbol that includes the line of early biblical patriarchs, Deists, materialists, cruelly castrating doublings of the same sex like Rahab and Tirzah — and mysteriously and irregularly sexual priests entering secret, curtained, erotically dark holy places. It is admittedly difficult to interpret Blake's meaning when he says that man "divides into Male & Female" when "the Individual appropriates Universality" (*Jer.*, 90:52–53; *E.*, 250). Is he saying that tyrannical Urizenic usurpation of the psyche leads to sexual quarrels? Or is he saying that humanity is lost when man regards himself exclusively or obsessively as a sexual animal? Or is he, as I believe, contrasting *natural* sexual division with the psychological *self*-division into "macho" male and coy female that occurs when man becomes more than man and plays God by demanding adherence to universalist dogma? To get an answer to these questions one must go back to the *Book of Urizen* and look at the coexistence of individual tyranny and sexual strife after the Fall. Here it must suffice to say that natural sexual division is a donnée of God, not only acceptable as a natural fact but for Blake an opportunity for vision. But *self*-division into sexual role-playing and excessive gender-commitment becomes psychological limitation. Such a fate is indeed what Blake goes on to predict: when

> the Male & Female
> Appropriate Individuality, they become an Eternal Death
> Hermaphroditic worshippers of a God of cruelty & law!
> [lines 53–55]

One or the other sex can erect itself into a hermaphroditic form — one sex hypostasized alongside the other, with sexual differentiation and attraction totally obliterated. Such a state Blake regards as hell.

I believe I have made clear from Blake's intellectual position why an androgynous ideal in any form is inappropriate for his vision of union between men and women. But I must confront an obvious difficulty which his visual art presents. The illustrations of the manuscript *Vala* show phalluses, vulvas, breasts, vaginas — all related to intersexual desiring — in grotesque and repulsive distortion; but in the ideal figures of Blake's finished art distinguishing sexual signs are often hard to determine. The disgust aroused by sexual organs in the state of perversion and sin should present no problem. *Pessimus corruptio optimi.* But can we conclude, from the often genitally sexless beings that float, rise, recline, leap upward with an aura of harmony and sweetness, that Blake

141

is banishing heterosexual desire as unworthy? Bodies revealing innocent natural life or engaged in commerce with eternity had in Western art traditionally been those of fairies, putti, or angels. This for obvious reasons: sexual identification, often denied these beings by sacred sources, would, in addition to being impious, have provided disruptive distractions from graceful movement and delicate meaning. Blake certainly did not want such distraction and may also not have wished to risk offending patrons and friends, many of whom were pious if not puritanical about sexuality and who would have responded more quickly to the overtly visual than to the indirectly suggestive verbal. And so his grotesque renditions of perverted sexuality in visual art are infrequent or faint or so obviously perjorative that they do not challenge his ideal, while his portrayals of men and women in ideal forms remain remarkably unsuggestive and chaste.

And yet in these latter the sense of body as body is unmistakable. Many of them are nude or nearly so, revealing bodily lineaments insistently though gracefully. And it is very easy to exaggerate the modesty. The nude risen Christ of the *Night Thoughts* illustration is not given a visible *membrum virile,* but it is more than implied behind his elevated knee in a bodily design that is completely human (Plate XVII). When Jerusalem, to take Blake's other ideal type (the female), is allowed to stand facing us, we see a lovely body unmistakably revealed, with full breasts and flaming hair (Plate XVIII). And in one of Blake's greatest works of art, his illustration to Dante's Circle of the Lustful (Plate XII), the bodies that rise into eternity remain fully physical though particular features are less distinct and obvious than in the states of generation and sin. The sweep into ultimate fulfillment in the great circular motions of this design is made not by individuals but couples.

After the hideous vision Blake has given us of sexual congress in the fallen world, it was understandable and tasteful that he should deemphasize overt physical representations of genitalia. But sexuality remains everywhere, and it is delicate because Beulah was ideally a place of gentleness blessed and instituted by the gentle Jesus.*

Perhaps no one can treat human sexuality adequately without being paradoxical, and Blake, like all the poets we have discussed, remained

---

*I risk here and elsewhere being accused of coming close to what Blake loathed, the "Yea Nay Creeping Jesus" of Blake's last surviving long letter (*E.,* 783). In *The Everlasting Gospel,* Blake portrays and defends an aggressively sexual Christ in origin and personal habit. This Christ I discuss in "Christ's Body" in *William Blake: Essays in Honour of Sir Geoffrey Keynes,* ed. Morton D. Paley and Michael Phillips (Oxford: Clarendon Press, 1973), 129–56, esp. 131–42. Here I want to emphasize the gentler qualities of the Beulah Christ.

PLATE XVII. William Blake, Frontispiece of Illustrations to Young's
Night Thoughts.

PLATE XVIII. William Blake, *Jerusalem*, plate 32, copy E.

committed to the view that human love was riddled with contrast and contradiction. But Blake was not one to run away from portraying a complex human condition or of erecting an ideal that was correspondingly rich in texture. He never deserted the view implied in the very earliest lyrics and prominent in the early prophecies that the ideal world was energized by physical contraction and expansion, by the pull and tug of opposing forces, by what Wallace Stevens has called the "polar circumstances" of the "imaginative life." But Blake also realized that here danger lurked. What Richard Ellmann has said about Stevens could be applied to Blake: "In the to-and-fro of magnified and minimized, the world might be lost." For the earlier poet, the harrowing reality of potential loss and distortion did not permanently dim the beauty and transforming power of what he early called "the Staminal Virtues of Humanity" (*E.,* 601), *virtue* here primarily bearing the older meaning of power but also, I think, suggesting possible goodness. Beulah preserved these powers in periods of great tribulation and kept them alive for imaginative exploitation. Indulgence in sexuality as pure pleasure Blake tended — realistically, properly — to separate from moments of intense mental concentration and creativity. But conscious recollection of sexual pleasure is available to imaginative experience, and it is one of Blake's many lessons for his own age and for posterity that such pleasure ought to enter more energetically and trenchantly into the structures of art and thought than it had in his own past and more mediately and elegantly than it has in our very recent sexual convulsions. Hence Eden and Beulah, though geographically distinct, Blake has made contiguous on his map of the mind as friendly neighboring realms.

5. PHILOSOPHICAL EPILOGUE
Nature and Imagination

Oh Love! no habitant of earth thou art—. . .
The mind that made thee, as it peopled heaven,
Even with its own deceiving phantasy,
And to a thought such shape and image given,
*   As haunts the unquench'd soul—parch'd—wearied—*
*   wrung—and riven.*
> Byron, *Childe Harold's Pilgrimage*, IV. 121 (*BCPW*, II, 164)

Is this to be A God   far rather would I be a Man
To know sweet Science.
> Blake, *FZ.*, 51:29–30; *E.*, 334

To live in the realm of forms does not signify an evasion of the
issues of life; it represents, on the contrary, the realization of one
of the highest energies of life itself. We cannot speak of art as "extra-
human" or "superhuman" without overlooking one of its funda-
mental features, its constructive power in the forming of our hu-
man universe.
> Ernst Cassirer, *An Essay on Man* (1953), 212–13

I divine that the true site of originality and strength is neither the
other nor myself, but our relation itself.
> Roland Barthes, *A Lover's Discourse* (1978), 35

All of the lexical and poetical constructions we have considered in the preceding pages involve both the imagination and nature. When Blake uses the simple adjective *sweet* in the climactic lines of one of his greatest visions, "the war of swords departed now / The dark Religions are departed & sweet Science reigns" (*FZ.*, 139:9–10; *E.*, 407), he also invokes these polarities of sense and mind. Samuel Johnson defined *sweet* both as "pleasing to any sense" and as "pleasing to the mind or spirit"; and Blake's meaning similarly ranges from the purely sensual (in his day "sweet in bed" bore obvious sexual meanings) to the highest reaches of intellect. Vastly different from *sweet* in origin and range of appeal is Coleridge's *co-adunation*, briefly considered earlier (see also *Notebooks*, no. 3154), but it erects the same polarities: the world of "finite Being" or Nature and the synchronic world of Imagination, primary and secondary. To "co-adunate" for Coleridge was to unite "Thought and Feeling in art" but also to unite the male and the female into the "music of pleasurable passion" (*Coll. Letters,* II, 865–66, 1034). The reconciliation of opposites works to produce the *tertium quid* both of friendship in life and of symbol in art.

Our subject has necessarily led us across frontiers into the realm of philosophy and aesthetics. The problem of what a nature-imagination symbiosis ultimately is strikes this commentator as philosophically insoluble. Can Paul Tillich's statement that there is "an element of 'libido' in all our aspirations" ever be proved? I would have to concede that some of the evidence for sexuality in the works discussed in this book has to be felt on the pulses, in the blood, along the heart and that some of the "argument" on previous pages has therefore been mostly display and presentation. When we get to the more rarefied matter of transcendence, the difficulty of ratiocinative comprehension increases, and Paul de Man has said rightly that the coincidence of imagery and natural object, of imagination and nature remains the "fundamental ambiguity" of Romantic poetics: "the tension between the two polarities never ceases to be problematic." From those tensions the ideal of fusion in love of sexual body and philosophic mind can scarcely be exempted.

Philosophers who stress only one or the other side of the nature-mind polarity are bound to disappoint us, and since such emphasis is almost inevitable, the reader should brace himself for encountering philosophical positions that fall short of a compelling intellectual formulation. Diderot came to believe, as did all the poets we have discussed, that physical love must be accompanied by tenderness if we are to attain the enjoyments that have been promised will attend the union of souls. But the powerful and unconventional individualism he recommended, with its free and uninhibited sexuality, tends to feed on a nature insufficiently checked by the philosopher's appeals to the common welfare or utility for the individual. And Diderot's Utopia, when it does not seem remote, looks dangerous or impractical. Conversely, thinkers like Archibald Alison (who seems to find no beauty in nature and matter alone but only in the "Expression of the Mind") or Thomas Holcroft (who made the mind the basis of all reality, endowing it with the power of altering even the structure of the body) make one cry out for the refutation which Samuel Johnson so memorably administered to Bishop Berkeley's idealism.

Such cautions as those given above are not entirely inappropriate as we look briefly at German philosophy and ask what light it can throw on love's body and soul in union. Kant totally separated sensuality, inevitably an abridgement of freedom, from the ethical imperative of the Pure Reason, keeping nature and mind discrete. Although in discussing the sublime and the beautiful early in his career he does leave some place for the polarities of masculine and feminine, the great syntheses of his maturity tend to evade the problems raised by our consideration of the Romantic body. Friedrich Schiller's famous definition of beauty as "living form" surely implies something about the sensuous and the sensual, which of course are present in the world of nature. But art's relationship to that world is the same as that of art to the purely didactic. Neither nature alone nor ethical formulation alone is satisfactory, and such dissatisfaction with the partial or initiatory is fully understandable. But can we similarly applaud Schiller's notion of the *tertium quid*? In his union of opposites, the earlier conditions—didacticism (or instruction) and natural passion—are alike destroyed: they disappear into the higher synthesis. "There is a fine art of passion, but an impassioned fine art is a contradiction in terms; for the inevitable effect of the Beautiful is freedom from passions." This is far from Hume's view: for him, as we have seen, beauty in life led to passion and benevolence, and one assumes that such links in life were not broken in good art. Certainly Schiller's definition is egregiously inconsistent with what we feel as powerfully present in Blake's, Shelley's, or Wordsworth's idealistic apocalypses, the palpable presence of an emotionally vivid and intense nature. Romantic poetic art does not seem to annihilate the reality of the body any more than it does didactic instruction, which remains allegorically present even in the most exalted symbol.

In the section from *The World as Will and Idea* (1819) quoted in the Preface of this study, Schopenhauer uses the word *beauty*, which is for him a key concept, as it had been for Schiller. But unlike Schiller, Schopenhauer keeps it electric with natural sexual energy. In some ways regressive and reactionary, he skips over the achievements of eighteenth-century sensibility in softening and sweetening love and so readying it for the marital nest; instead, he tries to return marriage to its ancient and exclusive procreative functions and deprives it of almost all else. Love grows from "immediate instinctive attraction," and it never loses its contact with sensual earth. There is some kind of transcendence even in this concentration on the basic urges, since the preservation and growth of the species is the most important matter with which mankind can possibly be concerned and is worthy of the sublimest poetry. But passion, the love of the species rather than of the individual, the essential will to live, does not frequently or easily co-exist with friendship; and Schopenhauer, who rejects homosexuality, androgyny, pederasty, also rejects the ideal of romantic union in love. His uncompromising naturalism separates him sharply from the great English Romantics, who were no more beguiled by bodily than by mental exclusiveness. In the relations of the sexes Schopenhauer stresses the importance of a straight figure, beautiful feet, a handsome face, good bones, and powerful instinctual drives — and little more. Erich Heller comments, acutely and wryly, that "it is the species that alone matters to the Will, the species and its procreation, excessively guaranteed by a superfluity of sex-craving entities."

Hegel is by all odds the philosopher of love most relevant to Romantic poets. Like Schopenhauer, he saw the great end and function of love-unions to be the living child, the child who unites the lovers who produced him and who becomes an "eternally self-developing and self-generating" body which bears within it a "seed of immortality." Hegel finds sublimity not only in the product but in the production, for in love-unions there is the beginning of the quest for universality. Ecstasy annuls all differences between the lovers — a view quite different from that of Swift, who found only selfishness in copulation; physical love for the philosopher displaces aloofness and singularity and begins the motion of the spirit toward transcendence. By insisting on sexual "deaths" to release spirit, Hegel recalls the incarnational beliefs of Blake, just as the faith that love drives on to a unity with the world and to the achievement of the *Ideal* recalls Shelley. Hegel, however, by denying to women, whom he found passive and subjective, the possibility of reaching the highest level, short-circuits the transcendence the English poet hoped to achieve in love and in strenuous collaboration with the opposite sex.

This last deficiency also seems to me to appear in Hegel's philosophy of fine art, which he believed had attained a kind of apogee in his own age, particularly in the poetry of Goethe: "Love is here wholly absorbed in the imagination"; desire and "enamourment" disappear in "a pure delight in the objects delineated, an inexhaustible self-absorption of imagination, . . . an intense jubilation of the soul in its own free movement." But such solipsistic mental satisfactions are not those of Keats, Wordsworth, and Blake, whose minds were in constant intercourse with the reality that originally and continuingly inspired them.

But if we go back in time to the Middle Ages and if we go down Hegel's dialectical ladder a few rungs from the *Ideal* to the *Ideel,* we do find an illuminating analogue to Romantic achievement. In high medieval art, as in the sex act, Hegel finds that affection, honor, fidelity unite to overcome personal selfishness and isolation and that aesthetic achievement, like the surrounding culture, was especially congenial to beauty and delicacy in love, qualities fostered by the feminine spirit of the age. Such an ideal, however, lacked what women themselves lack, a propulsion toward the very highest state of mind in which a new objectivity swallowed up, as in Schiller's synthesis, the disturbing particularities of experience. But on its own level the Hegelian *Ideel* has its peculiar beauty, quite apart from any historical period that he thought embodied it and certainly apart from the loftiest *Ideal,* which suffers from the blindnesses noted — limitations of vision about women shared by some of the Romantic poets. The *Ideel* could resist death, lead to free individual consent, achieve the truly ethical; it rested on sexual difference; it respected the mind; it attained intellectual significance; it moved toward the integrity of the personality; and the marriage that embodied it could achieve both the *rechtlich* and the *sittlich.* Such philosophy is as full a parallel as we are likely to find for the Romantic version of "esteem enlivened by desire."

However much the imagination may have tended to pull the spirit of the Romantic poets toward sublimity and exaltation, they for the most part resisted the kind of ultimate formulation that we have seen denied oxygen to the highest syntheses of Schiller and Hegel. It is not that the Romantics always remained close to human and empirical concerns — think of Shelley's taste for thin upper air, for example, or of Coleridge's occasional intellectual impenetrability. But it has been my thesis that they triumphed not only because they allowed life to freshen and sometimes even compromise ideality in its own naturalistic way but also because they were by heritage and belief committed to a more complicated way, not a *via negativa* but a secularized *via crucis,* in which bodies die but live again as bodies, in which Flesh impregnates Word. Like Paul, the Romantics did not want to be "unclothed" as much as they wanted to be "clothed upon"; they hoped that "mortality might be swallowed up of life" (II Corinthians 5:4). It is also true that, though naturalized and humanized Christianity remained a force, it was that very naturalizer and humanizer of established religion, the empirical Enlightenment, that itself also impinged upon the Romantic spirit, not least when it tried to express sexual love. It is precisely at this point that a modern critic, much preoccupied with Coleridge, becomes relevant. We have tended recently to lose sight of the contribution of I.A. Richards, though he is often referred to; one reason he can help us in understanding and evaluating Romantic idealization is that he developed a realistic and flexible view of the relations of nature and art. He saw that aesthetic experiences are "closely similar" to other experiences. Art provides "only a further development, a finer organization of ordinary experience" and is "not in the least a new and different kind of thing." Richards of course conceded that nature can be viewed as "a projection of our sensibility," but such a nature, "a Nature of our making," is "the deadest Nature we can conceive." Real need and real power come from less subjective places, and poetry must have ways of touching the earth to renew its strength. Full justice must of course be done to the creative powers of the projective imagination as it appears in Coleridge, Shelley, Blake, or Keats; but even these authors, if the emphasis of this book has been just, need to be seen from both below and above, particularly when they write of so clamorously a real and so insistently an ideal matter as love. Unlike some idealistic philosophers, they retained in their highest flights a view of the ground beneath.

Creative, energetic sensuality, which as an activity Blake separated from intense intellectual life, nevertheless energized his Eden, the realm of full personal integrity and relationship. The familiar Wordsworthian nest, the seed bed of his greatest poetry, was in fact a Beulah, a "married land" even before he brought to it a wedded wife, who had in one sense already been one of its denizens. Grasmere was a place of rest and retreat but also, as the poetry shows powerfully though indirectly, a place of sexual energy. That energy was paradoxically at its most efficacious for poetry when it was not fully expressed in life. But when Mary the wife succeeded Dorothy the sister and so permitted physical and emotional fulfillment of a very high order in the family, the poetry did remain amorously vital (though not so intensely vital as before) until the final freezing over. Wordsworth's "vital feelings of delight" (*PW.*, II, 15) were derived directly from nature, though they were of course mediated by his own naturally educated imagination. Keats ends by uniting his myth of love with nature, where it renews itself in the diurnal and seasonal cycles. More than any other Romantic, this poet of sensations and the imagination had begun as a purely mental traveler, his world being one created out of English Renaissance books and Italian Renaissance canvases. But he moved steadily toward life, and in that progress toward reality he gave us one of the intensest expressions of physical union ever written. And when his imagination came to its own creative rest, it settled comfortably in the warm, Beulah-like chamber of heterosexual love.

If in concluding I may return to the geographical metaphor used earlier, Blake's map of Eden and Beulah can be used to guide us into the sensibility of all the Romantic poets. Natural love borders closely upon the higher realm of imaginative creation, but it is distinct and separate, although not entirely independent. The commerce between these two states is brisk and mutually profitable, and tensions are by no means unknown. One state does not try to colonize or absorb the other, and the truly loving and productive Pilgrim of Eternity bears a dual citizenship.

NOTES AND GLOSSES

Preface

page vii **philosophers altogether."** *The World as Will and Idea,* tr. R.B. Haldane and J. Kemp, 3 vols. (London: Routledge & Kegan Paul, 1883, 1964), III, 338.

page vii **sexual impulse."** Ibid., III, 339.

page viii **stereotypes of civilization.** See Harry C. Payne, "The Eighteenth-Century Family: An Elusive Object" in *Eighteenth-Century Life* 5 (Winter 1978):48–61 and esp. 60, 61 and n.13.

page viii **language's referents."** *Eighteenth-Century Studies* 16 (Winter 1982–83):175.

page ix **man to earth,"** Wordsworth, "To my Sister," *PW.,* IV, 60.

Chapter 1

page 3 **other goods."** M.H. Abrams, *Natural Supernaturalism: Tradition and Revolution in Romantic Literature* (New York: Norton, 1971), 431.

page 3 **from on high.** See Frederick L. Beaty, *Light from Heaven: Love in British Romantic Literature* (De Kalb: Northern Illinois Univ. Press., 1971), xvi, xvii, and passim.

page 4 *first LP.* Quoted by Alan Bold, ed., *The Sexual Dimension in Literature* (London: Vision Press, 1982), p. 8 of Introduction.

page 4 **at any other time.** In an essay, "The Fate of Pleasure: Wordsworth to Dostoevsky," which I have loved for many years, Lionel Trilling perceives the boldness and centrality of the concept in Wordsworth and Keats and its diminished or changed status in subsequent cultures. See *Romanticism Reconsidered,* ed. Northrop Frye (New York: Columbia Univ. Press, 1963), 73–106.

page 4 **different nature."** James Boswell, *Life of Johnson,* ed. George B. Hill and L.F. Powell, 6 vols. (Oxford: Clarendon Press, 1934–64), III, 246.

page 4 **Woman of Pleasure."** James Boswell, *The Hypochondriack,* ed. Margery Bailey, 2 vols. (Stanford, Calif.: Stanford Univ. Press, 1928), II, 47 (no. 40 for Jan. 1781).

page 5 **prominent than ever.**   Frederick Antal, *Fuseli Studies* (London: Routledge & Kegan Paul, 1956), 90.

page 5 **had praised —**   Boswell, *Life of Johnson,* IV, 224.

page 7 **English painting";**   Hans Hess in Catalogue of Centenary Exhibit, City of York Art Gallery, 1941.

page 10 **voluptuous vitality."**   Bryan J. Bailey, *William Etty's Nudes* (Polloxhill, Bedford: Inglenook Publication, 1974), 47.

page 10 **no ascetic."**   Alexander Gilchrist, *Life of William Etty, R.A.,* 2 vols. (London, 1855), II, 323.

page 13 **sex of politics,"**   Quoted by Ronald Paulson, *Representations of Revolution (1789–1820)* (New Haven: Yale Univ. Press, 1983), 239.

page 13 **Sir Joshua."**   Ibid., 161.

page 13 **patriarchal society**   Ibid., 22.

page 13 **public nuisance."**   [Richard Cumberland], *The Observer: being a Collection of Moral, Literary and Familiar Essays,* 5 vols. (Dublin, 1791), I, 149.

page 13 **whole of Europe."**   Quoted by Devendra P. Varma, *The Gothic Flame* (London: Arthur Barker, 1957), 150.

page 14 **the temptation?"**   Matthew G. Lewis, *The Monk: A Romance,* ed. E.A. Baker (London: G. Routledge & Sons, 1929), 28 (Ch. 2).

page 15 **and fervid."**   Quoted by Varma, *Gothic Flame,* 143.

page 15 *Vathek* **his Bible,**   See Mario Praz's introductory essay to Peter Fairclough's edition of *Three Gothic Novels* (Baltimore: Penguin Books, 1968), 23.

page 16 **individual attachment."**   *The Friend,* ed. Barbara E. Rook, 2 vols., I (1969), 7, *Coll. Works* (Essay no. 1, 1818; the essay first appeared 1 June 1809).

page 16 **into wantonness."**   Varma, *Gothic Flame,* 148.

page 16 **Priapic worship**   R. P. Knight, *An Account of the Remains of the Worship of Priapus* (London, 1786).

page 17 **unblushing survey,**   Thomas Little, *The Beauty, Marriage-Ceremonies and Intercourse of the Sexes in All Nations, to which is added The New Arts of Love,* 4 vols., 2nd ed. (London, 1824). Parenthetical references to vol. and page are made in the text. The British Museum Catalog calls the author the Thomas Little of "the Opera Colonnade" and says his work is based on the *Kalogynomia.*

page 19 **divine energies."**   Thomas Taylor, *A Dissertation on the Eleusinian and Bacchic Mysteries . . .* (Amsterdam, 1790), 184.

page 19 **titillations of pre-puberty.**   For an illuminating discussion of pre-Oedipal, Oedipal, solipsistic, and polymorphous sexuality, see Barbara A. Schapiro, *The Romantic Mother: Narcissistic Patterns in Romantic Poetry* (Baltimore: Johns Hopkins Univ. Press, 1983).

page 20 **cuddly Savior.** Henry Rimius, *A Candid Narrative of the Rise and Progress of the Herrnhuters* (London, 1753), II, 40–41, 43–47.

page 20 **the Gospel,"** Archibald Alison, *Sermons, Chiefly on Particular Occasions,* 2nd Amer. ed. (Hartford, Conn.: 1815), 17, 19, 20.

page 20 **their [inflamed] senses."** Mary Wollstonecraft, *An Historical and Moral View of the Origins and Progress of the French Revolution and the effect it has produced in Europe* (London, 1794), I, 225–26; and *A Vindication of the Rights of Women,* ed. Charles W. Hagelman, Jr. (New York: Norton, 1967), 105.

page 20 **dissipated the physical,** see Jean H. Hagstrum, *Sex and Sensibility: Ideal and Erotic Love from Milton to Mozart* (Chicago: Univ. of Chicago Press, 1980), Index, *s.v. Angélisme* and also 270–71 and n.55.

page 21 **too precarious"—** Paul M. Zall, "The Cool World of Samuel Taylor Coleridge: Elizabeth Inchbald; or, Sex and Sensibility," *The Wordsworth Circle* 12 (Autumn 1981):270–73.

page 21 **passionate novels."** Juliet McMaster, *Jane Austen on Love,* English Literary Studies, no. 13, Univ. of Victoria (Victoria, B.C.: 1978), 16.

page 21 **"sumptuous destitution"—** Richard Wilbur's essay on Emily Dickinson is so entitled in *Responses: Prose Pieces: 1953–1976* (New York: Harcourt Brace Jovanovich, 1976), 3–15. I owe this reference to Professor and Mrs. James Gargano of Washington and Jefferson College.

page 24 **and "pleasing."** *Hypochondriack,* Essay 13 (Oct. 1778), I, 190. Boswell writes on love in nos. 11, 12, 13.

page 25 **gracious, mannerly.** See "A Letter from Mr. Burke, to a Member of the National Assembly; . . ." (1791) in *Works of . . . Burke,* VI (London, 1803), 37–38.

page 25 **in marriage.** See Hagstrum, *Sex and Sensibility,* 13, 26–34.

page 25 **a higher perfection."** Boswell, *Life of Johnson,* I, 382, and Johnson's *Sermons,* ed. Jean Hagstrum and James Gray, *Yale Works* (New Haven: Yale Univ. Press, 1978), XIV, 13.

page 25 **next to what."** Ronald Paulson, *Emblem and Expression* (Cambridge, Mass.: Harvard Univ. Press, 1975), 157. The entire ch. 8 of this work ("The Conversation Piece . . .") should be consulted. I have myself seen many conversations in many galleries and many photographic archives. I have also consulted the texts and reproductions of the following: Ellen G. D'Oench, *The Conversation Piece: Arthur Devis and his Contemporaries* (New Haven: Yale Center for British Art, 1980); Mario Praz, *Conversation Pieces* (University Park: Pennsylvania State Univ. Press, 1971); Ralph Edwards, *Early Conversation Pictures from the Middle Ages to about 1730* (London: Country Life, 1954); Ellis Waterhouse, *The Dictionary of British 18th Century Painters in Oils and Crayons* (Antique Collectors Club, 1981).

page 26 **and affection,"**   Paulson, *Emblem*, 123.

page 26 **young love."**   John Hayes, *Thomas Gainsborough* (London: Tate Gallery, 1980), 140, 142.

page 29 **and marriage.**   Hugh Honour, *Romanticism* (New York: Harper & Row, 1979), 253. Honour reproduces the Runge work.

page 31 **translation of 1620**   I am grateful to Professor James G. Turner for calling my attention to this lovely translation.

page 32 **not allay.**   See Norman Fruman, *Coleridge, the Damaged Archangel* (New York: George Braziller, 1971); Beverly Fields, *Reality's Dark Dream: Dejection in Coleridge,* Kent Studies in English, V ([Kent, Ohio]: Kent State Univ. Press, 1967); Lawrence S. Lockridge, *Coleridge the Moralist* (Ithaca, N.Y.: Cornell Univ. Press, 1977), 81, 84; Douglas Angus, "The Theme of Love and Guilt in Coleridge's Three Major Poems," *Journal of English and Germanic Philology* 59 (Oct. 1960):655–68.

page 32 **love and marriage.**   See Anthony John Harding, *Coleridge and the Idea of Love: Aspects of Relationship in Coleridge's Thought and Writings* (Cambridge, Eng.: Cambridge Univ. Press., 1974), passim; Jonas Spatz, "The Mystery of Eros: Sexual Initiation in Coleridge's 'Christabel,'" *Publications of the Modern Language Association* 90 (Jan. 1975):107–16.

page 33 **our nature. . . ."**   *Coleridge's Miscellaneous Criticism,* ed. Thomas M. Raysor (London: Constable & Co., 1936), 255.

page 33 **sex in our souls."**   *The Friend,* no. 16 (7 Dec. 1809), II, 209 in *Coll. Works*, IV.

page 33 **gradations of attachment"**   *Coleridge on Shakespeare,* ed. R.A. Foakes (Charlottesville: Univ. of Virginia Press, 1971), 92–94.

page 34 **perfectly spiritual."**   Ibid., 93.

page 34 **the Houyhnhnms":**   Quoted in Joseph A. Wittreich, ed., *The Romantics on Milton* (Cleveland: Press of Case Western Reserve Univ., 1970), 271.

page 34 **of Eve."**   Ibid., 201.

page 35 **every thing degrading."**   Ibid., 242.

page 35 **in the other."**   Ibid., 245.

page 35 **his friend's.**   See ch. 3, pp. 106–107.

page 35 **William Wordsworth.**   See ch. 3, pp. 96–97.

page 35 **sexual consummation."**   Brown, *Sexuality and Feminism in Shelley,* 58; see also 1, 24–25, and passim.

page 36 **social indifference."**   Jerome McGann,, *The Romantic Ideology* (Chicago: Univ. of Chicago Press, 1983), 118.

page 36 **sexual union.**   See ch. 2, pp. 54–55.

page 37 **pure, celestial."**   See Newman Ivey White, *Portrait of Shelley* (New York: Knopf, 1959), 392.

page 37 **Italian Platonics,"**   Ibid.

page 37 **of love**   Ibid., 394.

page 37 **flesh and blood."**   Cited by Carl Grabo in *The Magic Plant: The Growth of Shelley's Thought* (Chapel Hill: Univ. of North Carolina Press, 1936), 337.

page 37 **the Empyraean.**   Notably Earl R. Wasserman, *Shelley: A Critical Reading* (Baltimore: Johns Hopkins Univ. Press, 1971), 417–61. Kenneth Neill Cameron is a good corrective to strongly idealistic views of the poem, in which, he says, "the sexual imagery is obvious and intentional." *Shelley: The Golden Years* (Cambridge, Mass.: Harvard Univ. Press, 1974), 288.

page 37 **denying it."**   Grabo, *Magic Plant,* 342.

page 38 **a sexual idea";**   Joyce Carol Oates, "The Magnanimity of *Wuthering Heights,*" *Critical Inquiry* 9 (Dec. 1982), 447.

page 39 **to Cathy."**   J. Hillis Miller, *The Disappearance of God* (New York: Schocken Books, 1965), 195.

page 39 **once more.**   Oates, *Critical Inquiry* 9:447.

Chapter 2

page 41 **floundering cause."**   Cited by Oates in *Critical Inquiry* 9:435–36.

page 41 **too assured."**   Oates in Ibid., 436.

page 42 **spiritual vulgarity."**   F.R. Leavis, *Revaluation: Tradition & Development in English Poetry* (London: Chatto & Windus, 1936), 265.

page 42 **enchantingly sensuous."**   Matthew Arnold, Essay IV in *Essays in Criticism: Second Series* (London: Macmillan, 1935), 71.

page 42 **"anything else"**   Ibid.

page 42 **Lawrence Lipking**   Lipking, *The Life of the Poet: Beginning and Ending Poetic Careers* (Chicago: Univ. of Chicago Press, 1981).

page 43 **than to others."**   Christopher Ricks, *Keats and Embarrassment* (Oxford: Clarendon Press, 1974), 11.

page 43 **our first loves,"**   Quoted by William Walsh, *Introduction to Keats* (London: Methuen, 1981), 2.

page 44 **"sensate bosoms"**   Robert Merry, *The Florence Miscellany* (Florence, 1785–90), 69.

page 44 **turned in disgust,**   A review of Thomas Moore's *Epistles, Odes, and Other Poems* (1806) in the issue for July 1806 (8:458). See James A. Greig, *Francis Jeffrey* of The Edinburgh Review (London: Oliver and Boyd, 1948), 150.

page 44 **an abiding predilection.**   Morris Dickstein has perceived the innocence that dwells in the earliest Keatsian bower. The realm of Flora and old Pan is, he says, "overtly erotic, though with an innocence that recalls . . . the undifferentiated and instinctual fulfillment of childhood." *Keats and his Poetry: A Study in Development* (Chicago: Univ. of Chicago Press, 1971), 36.

page 44 **young John Keats.**   See Robert Gittings, *John Keats* (Boston: Little, Brown, 1968), 43.

page 48 **early Keats."**   John Jones, *John Keats's Dream of Truth* (New York: Barnes & Noble, 1969), 211.

page 48 **sexual relaxation."**   Walsh, *Introduction to Keats,* 16.

page 48 **heroic mode."**   See Lionel Trilling's edition of *The Selected Letters of John Keats* (Garden City, N.Y.: Doubleday Anchor Books, 1956), 2.

page 52 **Some have**   See Jack Stillinger, *The Hoodwinking of Madeline and Other Essays on Keats's Poems* (Urbana: Univ. of Illinois Press, 1971), 78.

page 52 **metaphysical critics**   Chiefly Earl Wasserman in *The Finer Tone: Keats' Major Poems* (Baltimore: Johns Hopkins Univ. Press, 1953). For a trenchant summary of the views of these critics, see Stillinger, *Hoodwinking,* 70–72.

page 52 **as a pander.**   Ibid., 72–81. Having presented a highly realistic reading in order to counter the idealists, Stillinger then goes on to qualify his own harshness, finding that Keats does in part identify with Porphyro. Ibid., 82–83.

page 52 **open-ended undecidability.**   See Anne K. Mellor, *English Romantic Irony* (Cambridge, Mass.: Harvard Univ. Press, 1980), 89–90.

page 54 **positions grotesque."**   Referred to by J.C. Furnas, "The Ant and the Twig or the Dark Side of God," *American Scholar* 53 (Winter 1983–84):68.

page 54 **great source**   see ch. 3, p. 75.

page 54 **pure delight,"**   *Coleridge on Shakespeare,* ed. Foakes, 85.

page 54 **Romantic movement"**)   *Friedrich Schlegel's* Lucinde *and the Fragments,* tr. with an introduction by Peter Firchow (Minneapolis: Univ. of Minnesota Press, 1971), 7. Reference is made in the text to the pages of the original German in the edition of 1918, published in Munich by S.B. Dietrich.

page 55 **its perfection."**   *Coleridge on Shakespeare,* ed. Foakes, 84. Coleridge is here commenting on *Romeo and Juliet.*

page 57 **or availability.**   See especially Nerval's *Sylvie: Recollections of Valois,* and *Aurélia: Life and the Dream* in *Selected Writings,* ed. and tr. Geoffrey Wagner (Ann Arbor: Univ. of Michigan Press, 1970), 49, 115.

page 57 **never ceasd,"**   Severn to R.M. Milnes, 6 Oct. 1845, in *The Keats Circle,* ed. Hyder Edward Rollins, 2 vols. (Cambridge, Mass.: Harvard Univ. Press, 1965), II, 129.

page 59 **profane Love."**   Ibid., 130.

page 59 **bodily appetite."**   Hume, "Of the amorous passion, or love betwixt the sexes," Part II, Book II, Section xi of *A Treatise of Human Nature.*

page 59 **point of view**   For this earlier point of view, see Jean H. Hagstrum, *The Sister Arts: The Tradition of Literary Pictorialism and English Poetry from Dryden to Gray* (Chicago: Univ. of Chicago Press, 1958), 161. For an archeological view of "unravish'd bride," see C.R.B. Combelback, "Keats's Grecian Urn as Unravished Bride," *Keats-Shelley Journal* 11 (Winter 1962), 14–15. See also William F. Zak, "To Try that Long Preserved Virginity: Psyche's Bliss and the Teasing Limits of the Grecian Urn," *Keats-Shelley Journal* 31 (1982):82–104, for the view that a knowing and even impish speaker, using a submerged sexual metaphor, accepts neither the lifeless Urn bride nor the final equation of truth and beauty.

page 60 **sculptured *biscuit.***   See Hagstrum's *Sex and Sensibility,* 180, 284, and Hagstrum, "Eros and Psyche: Some Versions of Romantic Love and Delicacy," *Critical Inquiry* 3 (Spring 1977): 521–42.

page 62 **Hazlitt celebrated.**   Both Hazlitt and Fuseli are quoted by Ian Jack in *Keats and the Mirror of Art* (Oxford: Clarendon Press, 1967), 210, 211.

page 63 **Tribes of *Mind"*)**   *Ode on the Poetical Character,* line 47.

page 67 **for non-being."**   Walsh, *Introduction to Keats,* 42.

page 67 **the "half"**   Leavis, *Revaluation,* 249.

page 68 **on to death,"**   See Jack Stillinger's textual edition, *The Poems of Keats* (Cambridge, Mass.: Harvard Univ. Press, 1978), 328, 638.

page 69 **the diasparactive**   I borrow the term from the fine study by Thomas McFarland, *Romanticism and the Forms of Ruin* (Princeton, N.J.: Princeton Univ. Press, 1981), 5 and passim.

Chapter 3

page 73 **giving in marriage,"** Quoted by Abrams, *Natural Supernaturalism,* 143.

page 73 **"ascetic" poet.** Ibid.

page 73 **Wordsworth's poetry,"** Leavis, *Revaluation,* 169.

page 73 **open tribute."** Carl Woodring, *Wordsworth* (Cambridge, Mass.: Harvard Univ. Press, 1968), 77.

page 73 **all-concealing tunic."** Shelley, *Peter Bell the Third,* IV, xi; VI, xix (*SPW.,* 354, 358).

page 73 **loves his friends"** Quoted by Ernest de Selincourt, "Wordsworth and his Daughter's Marriage," *Wordsworth and Coleridge: Studies in Honor of George McLean Harper,* ed. Earl Leslie Griggs (1939; rpt. New York: Russell & Russell, 1962), 79.

page 73 ***all* man"** Quoted by Derek Stanford in "Coleridge as Poet and Philosopher of Love," *English* 13 (Spring 1970):4. See Coleridge's often tortured comments implying or involving Wordsworth's sexuality, in the *Notebooks,* nos. 2998, 3146, and esp. 3148.

page 74 **and power.** *The Works of Thomas De Quincey,* 3rd ed., 16 vols. (Edinburgh, 1871), II, 144.

page 74 **source of life."** Geoffrey Hartman, "A Poet's Progress: Wordsworth and the *Via Naturaliter Negativa,*" reprinted from *Modern Philology* in the Norton Critical Edition of *The Prelude* (*Prel.,* 599, 604).

page 76 **of Imagination."** George Cheyne, *An Essay of Health and Long Life,* 2nd ed. (London, 1725), 159.

page 76 **Samuel Johnson's** See Jean Hagstrum, "Johnson and the *Concordia Discors* of Human Relationships," in *The Unknown Samuel Johnson,* ed. John J. Burke and Donald Kay (Madison: Univ. of Wisconsin Press, 1983), 39–53.

page 77 **the body."** Herbert Read, *Wordsworth* (London: Jonathan Cape, 1930), 13.

page 78 **was Annette."** F. W. Bateson, *Wordsworth: A Reinterpretation* (1954; rpt. London: Longmans, 1965), 88.

page 78 **by the war."** Emile Legouis, *William Wordsworth and Annette Vallon* (London: J.M. Dent & Sons, 1922), 59. Legouis adds that the poet's heart was "tormented by remembrance and remorse" (ibid.). Paul Sheats has said, justly, that Annette's influence was "intimately incorporated with that of the Revolution itself and . . . each liaison amplified and reinforced the other." *The Making of Wordsworth's Poetry, 1785–1798* (Cambridge, Mass.: Harvard Univ. Press, 1973), 75. Sheats also finds that Annette was "a contributory cause of the psychological crisis that did shape the poetry of 1797 and 1798." Ibid., 273, n.10.

page 79 **sexually alluring,** Kenneth R. Johnston recognizes "sexual and romantic undertones" in the tale of the Female Vagrant in the early version of *Salisbury Plain*. But is it necessary to believe that this sexual element in response to suffering is an example of a journalistic streak in Wordsworth, reacting to contemporary examples? The sexual had been in his sensibility from the beginning, as we have seen, and was peculiarly associated with suffering in his affair with Annette. See *Wordsworth and* The Recluse (New Haven: Yale Univ. Press, 1984), 44–45.

page 82 **fullest degree,"** Read, *Wordsworth,* 117.

page 82 **morbid repression."** Leavis, *Revaluation,* 169.

page 82 **thirteen to eight.** Cited by Abrams, *Natural Supernaturalism,* 295.

page 82 **"long-shut heart."** The phrases from Felicia Hemans come from Wordsworth's copy in the Huntington Library of her *Songs of the Affections* (Edinburgh and London, 1830), 3, 15, 17.

page 82 **and Imagination interlock,"** William Empson, *The Structure of Complex Words* (London: Chatto & Windus, 1964), 299; see also 293.

page 83 **to have recovered,** For illuminating discussions of how Wordsworth's poems heal and restore the mind after mourning and loss, see Geoffrey H. Hartman, "A Touching Compulsion: Wordsworth and the Problem of Representation," *Georgia Review* 31 (Spring 1983):345–61, and Peter J. Manning, "Reading Wordsworth's Revisions: Othello and the Drowned Man," *Studies in Romanticism* 22 (Spring 1983):3–28. Manning, however, also shows how the poetry sometimes embodies the conflict which it tries to calm.

page 83 **guilty or criminal.** See Jean H. Hagstrum, "Toward a Profile of the Word *Conscious* in Eighteenth-Century Literature," forthcoming in a collection of essays on literature and psychology, edited by Christopher Fox. For examples of *unconscious* in Wordsworth, see 1805 *Prelude*, I, 589; VI, 122; and 1850 version, XIII, 455 (*Prel.,* 58, 192, 299).

page 84 **affectionate heart."** These words are used to describe the Lake Poets by John Taylor Coleridge reviewing his uncle's *Remorse* in *The Quarterly Review* 11 (April 1814): 182. See Donald H. Reiman, ed., *The Romantics Reviewed* (New York: Garland, 1972), part A, vol. II, 818, 821.

page 84 **frailties of passion,"** Cited by Jack, *Keats and the Mirror of Art,* 281, n.41.

page 84 **'The DEV-V-VILS!'"** Ibid. See also 213.

page 84 **significant group."** McFarland, *Romanticism and the Forms of Ruin,* 148. For an illuminating discussion, see the entire third chapter.

page 85 **Wordsworth is"** Quoted by George Whalley in *Coleridge and Sara Hutchinson and the Asra Poems* (London: Routledge & Kegan Paul, 1955), 150.

page 85 **called polygamous.** Morris Golden, *Richardson's Characters* (Ann Arbor: Univ. of Michigan Press, 1963), 21, 22.

page 85 **"Affective Individualism"** Lawrence Stone, *The Family, Sex and Marriage in England 1500–1800* (New York: Harper & Row, 1977), 4 and passim.

page 85 **Irvin Ehrenpreis** *Acts of Implication* (Berkeley: Univ. of California Press, 1980), 136–37.

page 86 **domestic affections.** See the discussion by Karl Kroeber, "Constable: Millais/Wordsworth: Tennyson" in *Articulate Images: The Sister Arts from Hogarth to Tennyson,* ed. Richard Wendorf (Minneapolis: Univ. of Minnesota Press, 1983), 224–25.

page 86 **without articulation.** See Foucault, *History of Sexuality* and Roland Barthes, *A Lover's Discourse: fragments,* tr. Richard Howard (New York: Hill and Wang, 1978).

page 88 **Surely Herbert Read** *Wordsworth,* 218.

page 88 **Donald H. Reiman** "Poetry of Familiarity: Wordsworth, Dorothy, and Mary Hutchinson" in *The Evidence of the Imagination,* ed. Reiman, et al. (New York: New York Univ. Press, 1978), 168–70.

page 88 **former self."** Ibid., 170.

page 89 **"conjugal lewdness"** See Hagstrum, *Sex and Sensibility,* 102.

page 91 **her body.** Frank McConnell, *The Confessional Imagination: A Reading of Wordsworth's Prelude* (Baltimore: Johns Hopkins Univ. Press, 1974), 182.

page 91 **Herbert Read's** Summarized by Woodring (*Wordsworth,* 76).

page 96 **unbreakable fidelity."** Mary Moorman, "William and Dorothy Wordsworth" in *Essays by Divers Hands,* Transactions of the Royal Society of Literature, NS 37 (London: Oxford Univ. Press, 1972): 79.

page 96 **poetical circumstance")** Quoted by Beaty, *Light from Heaven,* 140.

page 98 **off symbolically."** Bateson, *Wordsworth: A Reinterpretation,* 153.

page 98 **Donald Reiman's**   Reiman, "Poetry of Familiarity," 158. Reiman sees the origin of the Lucy poems as lying in Wordsworth's unconscious attempt to avoid attaching his sexual drive to his sister. He shifts his stance from brother to lover, thus "fully utilizing their [the Lucy poems'] emotional energy by casting them as love poems."

page 101 **indeed to be.**   See Bruce Clarke, "Wordsworth's Departed Swans: Sublimation and Sublimity in *Home at Grasmere,*" *Studies in Romanticism* 19 (Fall 1980):355–74.

page 102 **Faithful Companions."**   See *Home at Grasmere,* MS. A, line 347, p. 127 and cancellation after line 351, p. 129; MS. B, lines 336, 347, p. 58; MS. D, lines 250, 261–62, p. 59.

page 102 **extreme attachments."**   John Beer, *Wordsworth and the Human Heart* (London: Macmillan, 1978), 164. See also the important comment of Kenneth R. Johnston in *Wordsworth and* The Recluse that throughout the history of *The Recluse* "the image of a 'happy band' secure in a snug cottage" is "a symbolic contrast and partial resolution to dislocated lives and ruined cottages in the world at large. . . ." (8).

page 104 **Wordsworth: chasm,**   On the funerary as well as the birth implications of "dread chasm" in Wordsworth's sonnet, "To the Torrent at the Devil's Bridge, North Wales, 1824," see Geoffrey H. Hartman, "Blessing the Torrent: On Wordsworth's Later Style," *Publications of the Modern Language Association* 93 (March 1978):199.

page 104 **gloomy blue"**   I quote here from the revised version of 1849, line 413 (*PW.,* I, 73). The 1793 version has merely "a gulf of gloomy blue" (line 498), which opens wide in a "mighty waste of mist," a "solemn sea" (lines 495–96, *PW.,* I, 72). I have been anticipated in drawing this parallel by Jonathan Wordsworth, with whose analysis I feel deeply sympathetic, though I go farther in drawing out physical and sexual meanings. J. Wordsworth wants to keep nature intact in this vision, finding the universe "humanized" and insisting that "the most noticeable feature of this landscape is that it is alive." "The Climbing of Snowdon" in *Bicentenary Wordsworth Studies in Memory of John Alban Finch,* ed. Jonathan Wordsworth (Ithaca: Cornell Univ. Press, 1970), 449–74, esp. 458, 461.

page 104 **a ghastly breach."**   Wordsworth, "After-Thought" (1832, 1837), line 7, *PW.,* III, 174.

page 105 **animal in us.**   See earlier this chapter, pp. 74–76.

page 106 **with admiration.**   See Hartman, *Wordsworth's Poetry,* 60–67, 122, 367, n.10. Hartman concedes hesitatingly that the vision on Snowdon possesses sexual energy and that the breach may have "sexual or birth-channel implications" (367, n.10).

page 108 **you have.** Quoted by Mary Moorman, "William and Dorothy Wordsworth," in *Essays,* 82.

Chapter 4

page 110 **of the other.** See Damrosch, *Symbol,* 185. Damrosch, for example, says that Blake "will not admit the necessary role of the 'other'" (179).

page 110 **to pass through,** Compare Damrosch, *Symbol,* 160: "For Blake childhood or Innocence is a state to pass through, not a permanent foundation for all later behavior."

page 111 **in broad daylight."** Diderot, *Supplement to Bougainville's "Voyage,"* 199 in *Rameau's Nephew and Other Works,* tr. Jacques Barzun and Ralph H. Bowen (New York: Bobbs-Merrill, 1964), 190.

page 114 **as did Blake.** Richard Payne Knight, *An Analytical Inquiry into the Principles of Taste,* 2nd ed. (London, 1805), 346–48, in Part III ("Of the Passions"). The 1st ed. appeared in 1805, the 4th in 1808, showing the popularity of this work.

page 123 **sweet and pleasant,"** *The Pilgrim's Progress,* ed. James Blanton and Roger Sharrock, 2nd ed. (Oxford: Clarendon Press, 1960), 154.

page 125 **forgiving mildness.** For an illuminating discussion of mildness as a Blakean concept, see Morton Paley, *The Continuing City: William Blake's Jerusalem* (Oxford: Clarendon Press, 1983), 66–69.

page 128 **keeps a mistress.** See Swedenborg, *The Delights of Wisdom Concerning Conjugial Love* (London, 1794), iii, 393, 398, 400, 424, 428, 430–31.

page 128 **as Cathedron;** See S. Foster Damon, *A Blake Dictionary* (Providence, R.I.: Brown Univ. Press, 1965), under the concepts mentioned.

page 132 **and arousal.** Hilton, "Some Sexual Connotations," 168. Hilton does, however, go on to quote the passage from *Milton* 35:24–25 (*E.,* 135) that shows that you cannot behold the beauty of Golgonooza, Blake's realm of art, "till you become a Mortal & Vegetable in Sexuality / Then you behold its mighty Spires & Domes of ivory & gold" (ibid.). It is here, on the absolute and basic necessity of sexuality, that the emphasis should finally rest.

page 133 **delight of joy."** Hilton, 168.

page 133 **to the loins.** W.J.T. Mitchell, *Blake's Composite Art* (Princeton: Princeton Univ. Press, 1978), 55, n.25.

page 133 **with both.** In a searching analysis of Blake's use of the image of the garment and of weaving, Morton D. Paley presents the radically different alternatives the human body provides. See "The Figure of the Garment in *The Four Zoas, Milton,* and *Jerusalem*" in *Blake's Sublime Allegory,* ed. Stuart Curran and Joseph Anthony Wittreich, Jr. (Madison: Univ. of Wisconsin Press, 1973), 119–39. See also Andrew Lincoln's sensitive account of the contradictions present in Beulah: "Blake's Lower Paradise: The Pastoral Passage in *The Four Zoas,* Night the Ninth," *Bulletin of Research in the Humanities* 84 (Winter 1981): 470–78. It is always important to remember how radically Blake revises common meanings (of innocence, for example); though he lowers the sacred number *three* in importance and embraces the equally sacred number *four* as the number for total integration, we must still retain a sense of the sacred about three, remembering how Blake's Christ blesses bodies and Beulah alike. See James Engell on the Pythagorean Tetractys and the Hebrew Tetragrammaton and their relation to Blake. *The Creative Imagination: Enlightenment to Romanticism* (Cambridge, Mass.: Harvard Univ. Press, 1981), 253–54.

page 134 **One scholar** The comments to be quoted are made by W.H. Stevenson in his edition of *The Poems of William Blake* (New York: Norton, 1972), 739.

page 134 **statically infallible,** See my article on "Blake's . . . God" in James Engell, ed., *Johnson and His Age* (Cambridge, Mass.: Harvard Univ. Press, 1984), 425–58.

page 135 **own body."** Northrop Frye, *Fearful Symmetry* (Princeton: Princeton Univ. Press, 1947, 1958), 273.

page 136 **perversely dominant."** Anne Mellor, "Blake's Portrayal of Women," *Blake: An Illustrated Quarterly* 16 (Winter 1982–83):148.

page 136 **partially "fogged,"** Alicia Ostriker, "Desire Gratified and Ungratified: William Blake and Sexuality," ibid., 164.

page 137 **"simply is."** Ibid., 163.

page 138 **that condition.** See Hagstrum, "Blake's . . . God."

page 138 **Robert Gleckner** In his review of Damrosch, *Symbol,* in *Studies in Romanticism* 21 (Winter 1982): 666–74. I am indebted to this piece for several insights.

page 139 **word *emanation,*** The word has unfortunate connotations for us but not Blake. We do not have to go back to Neoplatonism to find the word used honorifically. Knight in *Priapus* (1786), who may have influenced Blake's sexual imagery and who disliked Platonists in general, refers both to "the general emanation of the pervading spirit of God" (sexuality in nature) and also to animals and plants as the "actual emanations of the Divine Power" (49–50).

For a perceptive modern discussion of *emanation* and related matters, see Diana Hume George, *Blake and Freud* (Ithaca: Cornell Univ. Press, 1980), ch. 6 ("Is She Also the Divine Image?"), esp. 189, where George says, rightly, that "the masculine *as a quality* is as emanative as is the feminine."

page 140 **for Blake androgyny**   The belief that Blake's ideal was androgynous is so pervasive that I cannot here allude to the many scholarly commitments to this view. Suffice it to point out that Thomas R. Frosch, who has emphasized the importance of the senses for Blake, who sees clearly that "the primary creative forces of our world are men and women," and who understands that "renewal for Blake is not a transcendence but a reorganization of the given," yet finds the risen Albion to be androgynous. *The Awakening of Albion: The Renovation of the Body in the Poetry of William Blake* (Ithaca: Cornell Univ. Press, 1974), 10, 39, 82.

page 141 **irremediable confusion.**   G.E. Bentley, Jr., *Blake Records* (Oxford: Clarendon Press, 1969), 544.

page 145 **might be lost."**   Richard Ellmann, review of Peter Brazeau's book on Stevens in *New York Review of Books,* 24 Nov. 1983.

Chapter 5

page 146 **reaches of intellect.**   Here I am entirely indebted to Mark L. Greenberg, "Blake's Science," in *Studies in Eighteenth-Century Culture,* ed. Harry C. Payne (Madison: Univ. of Wisconsin Press, 1983), 127.

page 147 **be proved?**   Tillich is quoted by Richard Gravil in "Wordsworth's Ontology of Love in 'The Prelude,'" *Critical Quarterly* 16 (Autumn 1974): 238.

page 147 **to be problematic."**   Paul de Man, "Intentional Structure of the Romantic Image," *Romanticism and Consciousness: Essays in Criticism,* ed. Harold Bloom (New York: Norton, 1970), 66.

page 147 **dangerous or impractical.**   For a summary of Diderot's views on sexuality, see Marjorie Gottheimer, "Diderot: The Emergence of a New Individualism," *Enlightenment Essays* III (Summer 1972), 126–36.

page 147 **of the Mind")**   Archibald Alison, *Essays on the Nature and Principles of Taste* (Dublin, 1790), 381, 383.

page 147 **of the body)**   Thomas Holcroft, *Monthly Review* 10 (Jan. 1793):59.

page 148 **freedom from passions."**   Schiller, *On the Aesthetic Education of Man,* tr. Reginald Snell (New York: Frederick Ungar, 1977), 106. See also 89, 107.

page 148 **instinctive attraction,"** Schopenhauer, *World as Will,* III, 355.

page 149 **sex-craving entities."** Erich Heller, *The Ironic German: A Study of Thomas Mann* (Boston: Little, Brown, 1958), 59.

page 149 **of immortality."** Quoted by Abrams, *Natural Supernaturalism,* 176–77.

page 149 **free movement."** G.W.F. Hegel, *The Philosophy of Fine Art,* tr. F.P.B. Osmaston (London: G. Bell & Sons, 1920), 400. See also ibid., 337–45.

page 150 **enlivened by desire."** The phrase is James Thomson's. See Hagstrum, *Sex and Sensibility,* p. 13 and n.30. The discussion of Hegel is based on the following works, besides the one already cited: *Hegel's Philosophy of Right,* tr. T.M. Knox (Oxford: Clarendon Press, 1952), esp. 110–16, 261–63; *Hegel's Philosophy of Nature,* ed. and tr. M.J. Petry, (London: Allen and Unwin, 1970), III, 176, 209, 212; *Hegel's Philosophy of Mind,* tr. William Wallace (Oxford: Clarendon Press, 1971), 64–66, 76.

page 150 **kind of thing."** I.A. Richards, *Principles of Literary Criticism,* 5th ed. (New York: Harcourt, Brace, 1934), 16.

page 150 **can conceive."** I.A. Richards, *Coleridge on Imagination* (New York: Harcourt, Brace, 1935), 164.

BIBLIOGRAPHICAL ESSAY

General

Although *The Romantic Body* should not be regarded as a sequel to my *Sex and Sensibility: Ideal and Erotic Love from Milton to Mozart* (Chicago: Univ. of Chicago Press, 1980), the earlier and longer book is certainly relevant as general background and for certain topics like "Angel, *angélisme*"; "Delicacy"; "Innocence: frontier with experience" and also for such authors contemporary to the Romantics as Goethe and Austen and for an author like Rousseau, often regarded as himself Romantic (*s.v.,* Index). Although my emphasis here has been on nature and reality, one must never forget that what we are dealing with is the verbal mythologizing of love, and hence a work that discusses love in language and that relates it to power—from the Catholic confessional of post-Tridentine Europe to the psychoanalyst's couch is most welcome: Michel Foucault, *The History of Sexuality,* vol. I, tr. Robert Hurley (New York: Pantheon Books, 1978), the first in a series of volumes left incomplete with Professor Foucault's death in July 1984. The sensibility of the Romantics, particularly of Blake and Shelley, has sometimes been compared to Hindu thought and feeling, but the profound differences between the Indian perception of love and the Western, to which the writers treated here are closely related, appears from a study like that of Akhileshwar Jha, *Sexual Designs in Indian Culture* (New Delhi: Vikas Publishing House, 1979). The second volume of Irving Singer's monumental *The Nature of Love,* entitled *Courtly and Romantic,* was issued late in 1984 by the University of Chicago Press, along with the second edition of the first volume, *Plato to Luther.* The second volume discusses some of the authors covered in my book and deals fully with the relevant philosophers. Frederick L. Beaty's *Light from Heaven: Love in British Romantic Literature* (De Kalb; Northern Illinois Univ. Press, 1971) remains a standard guide, even more so since my study tends to emphasize the physical aspect while Professor Beaty gives to idealized love important, though by no means exclusive, emphasis. Gerald Enscoe in *Eros and the Romantics: Sexual Love as a Theme in Coleridge, Shelley and Keats* (The Hague: Mouton, 1967) carefully relates the theme of love to ideas of God and order; and, although he sometimes overemphasizes the traditional love-reason antithesis, he does perceive the centrality of physical sexuality.

Works on Coleridge and Shelley should be mentioned here because I have not given these authors intensive treatment. Anthony John Harding, *Coleridge and the Idea of Love: Aspects of Relationship in Coleridge's Thought and Writings* (Cambridge, Eng.: Cambridge Univ. Press, 1974) and Nathaniel Brown, *Sexuality and Feminism in Shelley* (Cambridge, Mass.: Harvard Univ. Press, 1979) have made unnecessary further intensive analysis of the theme in these authors, at least in so short a study as mine. Any reference to the works mentioned so far will be given in clear but abbreviated notation.

The theme in Byron needs to be given more thorough attention than it has so far received; my own essay is only the merest beginning: "Byron's Songs of Innocence: the Poems to 'Thyrza,'" *Evidence in Literary Scholarship: Essays in Memory of James Marshall Osborn,* ed. René Wellek and Alvaro Ribeiro (Oxford: Clarendon Press, 1979), 379–93. Byron's poetry is quoted from *Lord Byron: The Complete Poetical Works,* ed. Jerome J. McGann, 3 vols. (Oxford: Clarendon Press, 1980–81), abbreviated *BCPW.*). *Byron's Letters and Journals,* ed. Leslie A. Marchand, in 12 vols. including the index (Cambridge, Mass.: Harvard Univ. Press, 1973–82) are abbreviated *Byron LJ.*

Coleridge's poetry is quoted from *The Complete Poetical Works,* ed. Ernest Hartley Coleridge, 2 vols. (Oxford: Clarendon Press, 1912), abbreviated *CPWC;* and his prose, unless otherwise specified, from *Collected Letters of Samuel Taylor Coleridge,* ed. Earl Leslie Griggs, 6 vols. (Oxford: Clarendon Press, 1956–71), abbreviated *Coll. Letters*; from *The Notebooks of Samuel Taylor Coleridge,* ed. Kathleen Coburn, vols. I and II (New York: Pantheon Books, 1957, 1961) and vol. III (Princeton, N.J.: Princeton Univ. Press, 1973), each volume being a double one, with text and notes (references to these volumes will be abbreviated *Notebooks,* followed by the number of the entry); and from *The Collected Works of Samuel Taylor Coleridge,* 16 projected volumes with different editors under the general editorship of Kathleen Coburn (Princeton, N.J.: Princeton Univ. Press, 1971–), abbreviated *Coll. Works.*

Shelley's poetry is quoted from *Shelley: Poetical Works,* ed. Thomas Hutchinson (London: Oxford Univ. Press, 1967), abbreviated *SPW.*

Keats

The poetry is quoted from *John Keats: Complete Poetry,* ed. Jack Stillinger (Cambridge, Mass.: Harvard Univ. Press, 1982), abbreviated *CP.* The letters are quoted from *The Letters of Keats,* ed. Hyder Edward Rollins, 2 vols. (Cambridge, Mass.: Harvard Univ. Press, 1958), abbreviated *LK*. Helen Vendler, *The Odes of Keats* (Cambridge, Mass.: Harvard Univ. Press, 1983) is basic to any criticism of Keats; reference is clearly made in the text.

Wordsworth

The poetry is quoted from *The Poetical Works of William Wordsworth*, ed. E. de Selincourt alone for the first 2 vols. and with Helen Darbishire for the last 3 vols. (Oxford: Clarendon Press, 1940–54), abbreviated *PW*. *The Prelude* is quoted from *The Prelude 1799, 1805, 1850*, ed. Jonathan Wordsworth, M.H. Abrams, and Stephen Gill (New York: Norton, 1979), abbreviated *Prel*. For special reasons, some poems have been quoted from the Cornell Edition: *The Salisbury Plain Poems of William Wordsworth*, ed. Stephen Gill (Ithaca, N.Y.: Cornell Univ. Press, 1975), abbreviated *Salisbury Plain*; and *Home at Grasmere, Part First, Book First, of* The Recluse, ed. Beth Darlington (Ithaca, N.Y.: Cornell Univ. Press, 1977), abbreviated *Home at Grasmere*.

The prose is quoted from *The Prose Works of William Wordsworth*, ed. W.J.B. Owen and Jane Worthington Smyser, 3 vols. (Oxford: Clarendon Press, 1974), abbreviated *Prose*. The letters are referred to as follows: *The Letters of William and Dorothy Wordsworth: The Early Years*, ed. Ernest de Selincourt, 2nd ed., revised by Chester Shaver (Oxford: Clarendon Press, 1970), abbreviated *Letters Early*; *Letters: Middle Years*, Part II, ed. de Selincourt; rev. Mary Moorman and Alan G. Hill, 2nd ed. (Oxford, Clarendon Press, 1970), abbreviated *Letters Middle*; and *The Love Letters of William and Mary Wordsworth*, ed. Beth Darlington (Ithaca, N.Y.: Cornell Univ. Press, 1981), abbreviated *Love Letters*. Dorothy's journals are quoted from *The Journals of Dorothy Wordsworth*, ed. Ernest de Selincourt (London: Macmillan, 1959).

Basic to any discussion of Wordsworth are two important studies: M.H. Abrams, *Natural Supernaturalism: Tradition and Revolution in Romantic Literature* (New York: Norton, 1971), essentially a treatment of love in its largest meaning as inspiration, metaphor, and analogue for the union of mind and nature; and Geoffrey Hartman, *Wordsworth's Poetry 1787–1814* (New Haven: Yale Univ. Press, 1964), a treatment of the mythologizing, mediating, and universalizing mind of the poet.

Blake

Blake is quoted from *The Complete Poetry and Prose of William Blake*, newly revised, ed. David V. Erdman, with commentary by Harold Bloom

(Garden City, N.Y.: Anchor Press/Doubleday, 1982), abbreviated *E.* with the following abbreviations used for particular poems: *Amer.* for *America, FZ.* for *The Four Zoas, Jer.* for *Jerusalem, MHH.* for *The Marriage of Heaven and Hell, VDA.* for *The Visions of the Daughters of Albion.*

Frequent reference is made to Leopold Damrosch, Jr., *Symbol and Tradition in Blake's Myth* (Princeton, N.J.: Princeton Univ. Press, 1980), abbreviated *Symbol.*

INDEX

The Hodges Lectures

THE BETTER ENGLISH FUND was established in 1947 by John C. Hodges, Professor of English, The University of Tennessee, 1921–1962, and head of the English Department, 1941–1962, on the returns from the *Harbrace College Handbook,* of which he was the author. Over the years, it has been used to support the improvement of teaching and research in the English Department. The Hodges Lectures are intended to commemorate this wise and generous bequest.

THE HODGES LECTURES book series is set in ten-point Sabon type with two-point spacing between the lines. Sabon is also used for display. The series format was designed by Jim Billingsley. This title in the series was composed by Metricomp of Grundy Center, Iowa, printed by Thomson-Shore, Inc., Dexter, Michigan, and bound by John H. Dekker & Sons, Grand Rapids, Michigan. The paper on which the book is printed bears the watermark of S.D. Warren and is designed for an effective life of at least 300 years.

THE UNIVERSITY OF TENNESSEE PRESS : KNOXVILLE